YESHUATEKANI

THE ROSE OF SHARON AND LILY OF THE VALLEY

DAVID ALBERT JAMES BRAND

Copyright © 2025 David Albert James Brand.

All rights reserved. No part of this book may be reproduced, stored, or transmitted by any means—whether auditory, graphic, mechanical, or electronic—without written permission of both publisher and author, except in the case of brief excerpts used in critical articles and reviews. Unauthorized reproduction of any part of this work is illegal and is punishable by law.

ISBN: 979-8-89419-641-1 (sc)
ISBN: 979-8-89419-642-8 (hc)
ISBN: 979-8-89419-643-5 (e)

Because of the dynamic nature of the Internet, any web addresses or links contained in this book may have changed since publication and may no longer be valid. The views expressed in this work are solely those of the author and do not necessarily reflect the views of the publisher, and the publisher hereby disclaims any responsibility for them.

One Galleria Blvd., Suite 1900, Metairie, LA 70001
(504) 702-6708

CONTENTS

Chapter 1: Introduction & A Historical Analysis Of Deception In Christianity 1
Overview of the author's journey with bipolar disorder.
The importance of sharing these spiritual discoveries.
Introduction to Yeshuatekani as the central figure.

Chapter 2: Theological Analysis Of The Second Coming 3
Biblical references to the timeline of the Second Coming.
The significance of 1948 and the generational prophecy.
Discussion of current events as signs of the end times.

Chapter 3: Title's Of The Father's Names 9
Examination of "IEUE" as the Father's true name.
The origins and inaccuracies of "God" and "LORD".

Chapter 4: The Messiah's Name Above All Names 13
The significance of 'I AM' in the scripture
The discovery of Psalm 35: 3
The importance of Messiah's true name

Chapter 5: A Perspective On Yeshuatekani: The Female Messiah 17
Scriptural evidence of Yeshuatekani's femininity.
Theological implications of a female savior.
Analysis of references to breasts, female lamb offerings, and prophecy symbolism.

Chapter 6: Prophecies Of The Female Messiah: Yeshuatekani 27
The Rose of Sharon and the Lily of the Valley.
Song of Solomon as evidence of Yeshuatekani's identity.
Other Messianic prophecies tied to a female savior.

Chapter 7: The Wisdom Of Yeshuatekani 43
Personification of Wisdom as female in Proverbs.
Connections between Wisdom and Yeshuatekani.

Chapter 8: The Man Of Lawlessness 47
Identification of the pope as the "man of lawlessness".
Analysis of changes to Sabbath laws and Ten Commandments.
How modern Christianity deviates from Scriptural truth.

Chapter 9: The Restoration Of The Truth 59
The importance of recognizing Yeshuatekani as the true Messiah.
Steps to realign worship with Biblical instructions.
The significance of keeping Sabbaths and festivals.

Chapter 10: Building The Calendar 83
Call to action for believers.
Hope and preparation for the Second Coming.

BIBLE SUBSTITUTIONS

The Following Substitutions are made in Bible Verses quoted in verses in this book. Most of the substitutions are due to pagan names and titles. Thanks to C.J. Koster's book "Come Out of Her My People". It is a highly recommended read.

https://isr-messianic.org/publications/come-out-of-her-my-people.htm

Elohim – God
IEUE – LORD
Yeshuatekani – Jesus
Messiah – Christ
Master – Lord
Set-Apart Spirit – Holy Spirit
Set-Apart – Holy
Deliverance – Salvation
Esteem – Glory
Favor – Grace
Taught Ones – Disciples, Apostles
Impale – Crucify
Stake – Cross
Messenger – Angel
Baptize – Immerse

CHAPTER ONE

Introduction

A Historical Analysis Of Deception In Christianity

The last twenty-three years I have been living my life with a bipolar diagnosis. I have had some severe manic episodes and even more debilitating depressions.

During my illness I started studying the Scriptures and over time I made notes of things I found. This short book relays some of those discoveries. It is not a finished product but I felt it important to get the knowledge I have out there as soon as possible.

We live in the World of The Lie as many in the United States live in a Partisan "U versus Us" Political System where many votes are controlled by Republican party candidates who have endorsed and or convinced their constituents that President Donald Trump is our leader. This concept of leadership came to become known as the LIE or big lie.

There is a bigger lie about to unfold in Christianity. The Christian Savior is described as being a white man called Jesus. The real Savior is a black woman called **"Yeshuatekani"** and she will be working the world's stage no later than 15-May 2028.

How is it possible that Jesus was documented as male? Well, the culprit is Satan as the two verses below show. He deceives the whole world. Revelation was distributed sometime between 81 AD and 96 AD. So what is it that deceives and seduces the entire inhabited world. Certainly a man called Jesus replacing Yeshuatekani a female gendered Messiah qualifies.

__KJV Rev 12:9__ "And the great dragon was cast out, that old serpent, called the Devil, and Satan, which deceiveth the whole world: he was cast out into the earth, and his angels were cast out with him."

__AMP Rev 12:9__ "And the great dragon was thrown down, the age-old serpent who is called the devil and Satan, he who continually deceives and seduces the entire inhabited world; he was thrown down to the earth, and his angels were thrown down with him".

Major Deceptions

Influencing the translation processes to replace the Messiah with a man called Jesus.

Influencing the full-scale worship of Jesus and Miryam statues in blatant disregard of the 2nd Commandment. This exercising of idolatry is prevalent all over the world.

Establishment of Sunday Sabbaths plus a host of Christian Festivals (Easter and Christmas) in reckless disobedience of the 4th Commandment. Elimination of ALL of the Fathers Appointments.

We have only a short period of time before we meet the female Yeshuatekani and to identify the man of lawlessness and stop attending Sunday and other Christian Sabbaths.

CHAPTER TWO

Theological Analysis Of The Second Coming

THE Scroll of Revelation begins with Yeshuatekani giving revelations to the Taught One Yohannon to be shared with Yeshuatekani's servants. We are told that these prophecies are "to take place with speed". The second last paragraph of Revelation confirms once again "that yes I am coming speedily."

In 2 Kepha (Kepha was Peter's Name) we are told that mockers will come in the last days as disbelievers walking in their own lusts or sins and saying, "Where is the promise of Yeshuatekani's coming?" Kepha summarizes that the heavens and the earth are being kept for fire, a day of judgment for the destruction of sinners and the wicked.

It's 2023, almost over 2000 years since Yeshuatekani walked the earth and ascended into heaven. Where's the speed in that amount of time? No wonder there are scoffers and disbelievers but one of IEUE's definitions of time is "One day is as a thousand years and a thousand years as one day."

We are also told in Scripture that we cannot pick the hour or the day of the Second Coming. Only Father IEUE knows. However we can pick the generation that will see the end times. We are in that generation right now; every one of us is part of this living prophecy.

Yeshuatekani was impaled upon a stake, put in a tomb and rose again on the third day. In terms of 1000 years we are as of the year 2024 the beginning of the third day 2030 or so. One might think it makes sense then that Yeshuatekani The Messiah will return to earth on the 3rd day of a thousand years. However there is a hidden prophecy that gives us the exact generation that will see the Second Coming.

In Jeremiah the prophet was shown two baskets of figs. One basket had perfectly edible figs and the other had spoilt inedible figs. IEUE (The Father) then told Jeremiah that the basket of good figs represented people that He was going to make his own saying "they shall be My people and I shall be their Elohim (God), for they will turn back to Me with all their heart."(The Scriptures)

The baskets of spoilt figs were for those who were evil that IEUE was going to punish. He goes onto say "And I shall make them a horror to all the reigns of the earth".

I have heavily summarized Jeremiah 24 but all I wanted to illustrate was that good figs equal IEUE's servants and spoilt figs represent his enemies. In today's terms the Fig Tree symbolizes Israel.

In the Messianic Scriptures in Matthew 21 Yeshuatekani is travelling back from Bethany to Jerusalem and comes upon a fig tree with leaves but without any fruit representing the current state of Jerusalem and Israel who were opposed to Yeshuatekani. Yeshuatekani said to the Fig Tree "Let no fruit grow on thee hence forward for ever. And presently the fig tree withered away." This action prophesized that Israel would turn against Yeshuatekani and then be destroyed.

Within 40 years or so the withering fig tree of Jerusalem and Israel was destroyed and Jewish people were scattered into the gentile nations.

Later on in Matthew Chapter 24 Yeshuatekani extensively shares many elements of the end times with the Taught One's. Then Yeshuatekani gives us a parable telling us when these end times would occur. Yeshuatekani says, "Now learn a parable of the fig tree; When it's branch is yet tender, and puts forth leaves, ye know that summer is nigh. So likewise ye, when ye shall see all these things, know that it is near, even at the doors. Verily I say unto you, this generation shall not pass, till all these things be fulfilled."(KJV).

When did the Fig Tree (Israel) tender new leaves. Wikipedia gives us the answer: https://en.wikipedia.org/wiki/Israel

The end of the British Mandate for Palestine was set for midnight on 14 May 1948. That day, David Ben-Gurion, the Executive Head of the Zionist Organization and president of the Jewish Agency for Palestine, declared "the establishment of a Jewish state in Eretz Israel, to be known as the State of Israel.

So, those in the generation that will see the end time fulfilled is the generation that began in 1948. How long is a generation? Well if we base it on the average life expectancy of people which in Israel is 82 we can project 2030, very close to the beginning of the third (1000) day.

However it is always best to use Scripture when we can to come up with a much more accurate time frame, which strongly suggests the end days, are nearer. I believe that "A prayer by Mosheh (Moses)" gives us the evidence to define what a generation is.

Psalm 90:10 (KJV)

The days of our years are threescore years and ten(70 years); and if by reason of strength they be fourscore years(80 years), yet is their strength labor and sorrow; for it is soon cut off, and we fly away.

Mosheh died when he was 120 years old, so the generation in his prayer applies to the end times. Most scholars believe that this Psalm was the only one authored by Mosheh. Mosheh delivered IEUE's people to the Promised Land and Yeshuatekani will lead IEUE's servants to the Sovereigdom on earth with Jerusalem at its center.

The wrath of IEUE as described in the Scroll of Revelation shows tremendous suffering coming to earth. Yeshuatekani said that "And except those days should be shortened, there should no flesh be saved: but for the elect's sake those days shall be shortened."

So the verse "The days of our years are threescore years and ten (70 years); and if by reason of strength they be fourscore years (80 years), yet is their strength labor and sorrow; for it is soon cut off, and we fly away." Tells us that a generation starts at 70 but is extended to 80 years if we have the strength to make it through the tribulation. Thus a generation is 70 to 80 years with the period between 70 and 80 encompassing the last days and the Second Coming.

Thus 1948 + 70 = 2018

And 1948 + 80 = 2028.

Since this timeframe is a function of Scripture one may believe very strongly that we will endure the end days in that period of time. 05/14/2018 to 05/14/2028. Thus **Yeshuatekani** Will be on earth in our lifetime and judgment of you and I will begin.

We should note that **Mosheh** and **Yeshuatekani** are the two redeemers of Israel, thus the prayer of Mosheh is important and addresses the end times.

We should be happy and joyful that The Second Coming is just around the corner. However, Satan has deceived us so we have little time to get our act together and become true believers and worship IEUE in the appropriate way. Satan also knows his time is short so we can expect the world to begin collapsing and heading towards destruction and that he will do everything he can to make us become believers in "**The Man of Lawlessness – The Head of the Papacy – The Pope**".

It is fair to say that we are in the end times period described as the tribulation which is outlined in the Scroll of Revelations. I do not think it is merely coincidence that President Donald Trump's Name relates to the Seven Trumpets of Elohim's wrath as described in the Scroll of Revelation. Donald Trump probably set the Trumpets in motion in his first term as president and we are firmly in the grips of the tribulation the period of the end times. In his second term he will be partly responsible for the Seventh Trumpet – **the coming of Yeshuatekani.**

The TV News is a constant reminder that disasters, wars, plagues (Covid-19) are breaking out everywhere at an accelerating pace. The Scriptures describe the events we are witnessing as being the beginning of birth pains with catastrophic events occurring faster and faster and with increasing intensity. We who follow the news are all a witness to these escalating events from COVID-19, to Forest Fires, to Hurricanes and Tornados of increasing intensity and to violence which runs ramparts in our streets. It is easy to see that we are in the end times.

CHAPTER 3

Title's Of The Father's Names

THE FATHER'S NAME

God is not the Father's Name. Let's look at a summary of C.J. Kosters "Come Out of Her, My People" Pages 53-57. Gad is a Syrian or Canaanite deity of good luck or fortune. In Hebrew, it is written GD, but with Massoretic vowel-pointing, it gives us "Gad." Other Scriptural references to a similar deity, also written GD, have a vowel-pointing giving us "Gawd" or "God." Gad is identified with Jupiter, the Sky-deity or the Sun-deity. The word "God (or god)" is a title, translating the Hebrew **Elohim** (or elohim), El (or el), and **Eloah**.

Satan has replaced the Title "Elohim" with a pagan entity "God". Elohim means "Strong One or Mighty One". In Indo-Germanic dictionaries, only one word resembles "god." It is ghodh and is pronounced the same. This word means union, also sexual union or mating. According to Luneburger Wörterbuch, the following are the same word: Gott, got, gode, gade, god and guth (gud).

Elohim has two names mentioned in Exodus 3:14-15. One is "I Am" (Hebrew "Ehyeh". Ehyeh is seldom used as the other name is termed "The Father's Forever Name For All Generations". In the majority of

Bible Translations this Hebrew name "YHWH" is translated as the pagan sourced "LORD".

LORD can be sourced to pagan identities

(1) **Larth** who was an Estruscan house deity.

(2) **Loride** who was a Teutonic war deity

(3) The third potential source is predicted **Lordo** or **Lordon** who was another deity.

The Father, even his name would be substituted by a pagan entity.

Jeremiah 23:26-27 (KJV) *How long shall this be in the heart of the prophets that prophesy lies? Yea, they are prophets of the deceit of their own heart; Which think to cause my people to forget my name by their dreams which they tell every man to his neighbor, as their fathers have forgotten my name for Baal.*

Wikipedia shows us how LORD has a connection to Baal. The Northwest Semitic languages—Ugaritic, Phoenician, Hebrew, Amorite, and Aramaic—were all abjads, typically written without vowels. As such, the word ba'al was usually written as BʿL (bet-ayin-lamedh); its vowels have been reconstructed. In these languages, ba'al signified "owner" and, by extension, "lord", a "master", or "husband". It also appears as Baʿali or Baʿaly, "my Lord".

The underlying Hebrew Scrolls have "YHWH" instead of "LORD". "YHWH" is known as the Tetragrammaton name. There is great debate as to which vowels should be used to determine what the Father's name is. Yahway, Yehwey, Yahuweh and others are all subject to speculation.

What we should realize is that current Hebrew Scrolls are written in modern Hebrew. Ancient Hebrew includes vowels. This has resulted in the name "IEUE" being translated to modern Hebrews "YHWH"

"IEUE" is pronounced [Aay-Air-Ooh-Air] and his name likely means "He secures breathing."

CHAPTER 4

The Messiah's Name Above All Names

The name used in the vast majority of translations and on the tip of almost all Christians tongues is Jesus Christ. The name Jesus is sourced in paganism. The Greek documents underlying most of the English Translations have "Iesous" as the name of the Messiah.

"Iesous" in turn was derived from "Iaso" the Greek goddess of healing. Thus, the name "Jesus" doesn't have Hebrew roots and instead is of Greek Mythology specifically a female goddess. Why? The Greeks wanted to convert as many of their culture to the Messianic Faith as possible. By using their own god Iaso instead of the Messiah they would have more conversion success. They looked through their pantheon of gods and found that the god that most resembled the Messiah was the goddess Iaso. Iaso was chosen by the Greeks because the Messiah is female.

Isa is the Islamic name for The Messiah. It's awfully close to Iaso and Isa is also a unisex name. Let's continue our journey to the name. One clue is we know from John 5:43 KJV "I am come in my Fathers Name." The Father's two main names are "I am" and "IEUE". The Messiah is called many "I am's" in Scripture: "I am the bread of life","I am the light of the world", "I am from above", "I am Sovereign of the Yehudah", "I am the true vine", "I am the Alpha and Omega", "I am the first and the last", "I am the Rose of Sharon and the Lily of the Valley" and others.

With all of those "I Am's" I assumed that The Messiah came in the "I Am" Name. Another clue for the name is provided in Matthew 1:21 where we are told that the Name is based on "will save people from their sins".

My next step was to search the Pre-Messianic Scriptures (Old Testament) for a match on "I am savior", "I am deliverer" and "I am salvation" then look at the underlying Hebrew and see if it delivers a name. I used Bible Gateway to search the Scriptures for the above search items. I found only one match that qualified.

"I am thy salvation" in Psalm 35:3.

"Draw out also the spear, and stop the way against them that persecute me: say unto my soul, I am thy salvation."

Next, I used Strong's Lexicon on Biblehub.com to look at a detailed breakout of the "I am your salvation" showing the Hebrew equivalents of the English words.

"I [am]   אֲנִי: ('ā·nî)

Pronoun - first person common singular

Strong's Hebrew 589: 1) I (first pers. sing. -usually used for emphasis)

Your salvation."   יְשֻׁעָתֵךְ, (yə·šu·'ā·têḵ)

Noun - feminine singular construct | second person feminine singular

Strong's Hebrew 3444: 1) salvation, deliverance 1a) welfare, prosperity 1b) deliverance 1c) salvation (by God) 1d) victory

Looking at Strong's Hebrew 3444:

Yeshuah: salvation

Part of Speech: Noun Feminine

Transliteration: Yeshuah

NASB Lexicon

"I am your salvation."   יְשׁוּעָתֵךְ

                                   (ye·shu·ʾa·tech)

Yeshuatek + Ani = Yeshuatekani

How important is the Name? Phillippians 2:9 tells us the Messiah's Name is Above All Names

CHAPTER 5

A Perspective On Yeshuatekani: The Female Messiah

YESHUATEKANI

Yeshuatekani's Gender is *Female*

A number of observations are presented the sum total of which prove her female gender.

> The Oneness of the Image of **Elohim**
> Image of Elohim.

Genesis 1:26 (Based on KJV)

And Elohim said, "Let us make man in our image, after our likeness: and let them have dominion over the fish of the sea, and over the fowl of the air, and over the cattle, and over all the earth, and over every creeping thing that creepeth upon the earth".

Forty-Five English Translations on www.biblegateway.com use "Us" and "Our" or something equivalent confirming that "Us" and "Our" means more than One.

What is the Image?

Genesis 1:27 (Based on KJV)

So Elohim created man in his own image, in the image of Elohim created he them; male and female created he them.

The Image is "Male" and "Female". The "Us" and "Our" in the first verse above confirms that Elohim are male and female. The image becomes one when:

Genesis 2:24 (KJV)

"Therefore shall a man leave his father and his mother, and shall cleave unto his wife: and they shall be one flesh."

John 10:30 (KJV)

Yeshuatekani teaches us that she and the Father are a unity of one. **"I and my Father are one". John 10:30**

The Image of Elohim is male and female with the male being the Father and the female being the Messiah. As in marriage they are one.

In Indo-Germanic dictionaries, only one word resembles "god." It is ghodh and is pronounced the same. This word means union, also sexual union or mating and fits Elohim (God) to a "T".

Genetically Speaking

"Set-Apart" is used instead of Holy because (as C.J. Koster-Come Out Of Her My People expounds). The Hebrew word qodesh and the equivalent Greek word hagios and their derivatives have been translated as holy, hallowed, or sanctified in older English versions, and in modern versions as sacred. Bible dictionaries state that the meaning of qodesh (as well as qadash) specifies "separation." Modern scholars use the words "Set-Apart," "set-apart," and "apartness."

According to Dictionary of Mythology Folklore and Symbols, the following is stated about the word HOLY: In practically all languages, the word "holy" has been derived from the divinely honored sun. According to Encyclopedia of Religions, HOLI is the Great Hindu spring festival, held in honor of Krishna, as the spring sun-god.

"Holy" is rooted in paganism, another of Satan's deceptions.

Matthew 1:18 (Based On KJV)

"Now the birth of Yeshuatekani Messiah was on this wise: When as Her mother Miryam was espoused to Yoseph, before they came together, she was found pregnant with a child by way of the Set-Apart Spirit."

The Set-Apart Spirit is Spirit and is not physical. The Set-Apart Spirit does not have any semen. This is important because in a physical act of conception we need to pair up our 23rd set of chromosomes.

Each of us have 46 chromosomes arranged in 23 pairs. The 23rd chromosome pair determines the gender of a baby child. The gender of a child is determined by an XX or XY chromosome intersection between the parents. A man's 23rd chromosome consists of an X and a Y. A woman's 23rd chromosome consists of two "X"s. During love making if conception occurs and if a man's "X" joins a woman's "X" a baby girl will be born. If a man's "Y" joins a woman's "X" a baby boy is born.

From a genetic perspective Miryam had only "X" chromosomes available to her thus only a baby girl was physically possible.

The Female Lamb of Elohim: A Sin Offering

John 1:29 (Based on KJV)

"The next day John seeth Yeshuatekani coming unto him, and saith, Behold the Lamb of Elohim, which taketh away the sin of the world."

Before Yeshuatekani's impalement the Israelites made sin offerings to IEUE.

Here is a description of the process:

Leviticus 5:5-7 (Based on KJV)

"And it shall be, when he shall be guilty in one of these things, that he shall confess that he hath sinned in that thing: And he shall bring his trespass offering unto the IEUE for his sin which he hath sinned, a female from the flock, a lamb or a kid of the goats, for a sin offering; and the priest shall make an atonement for him concerning his sin. And if he be not able to bring a lamb, then he shall bring for his trespass, which he hath committed, two turtle doves, or two pigeons, unto the IEUE; one for a sin offering and the other for a burnt offering."

Leviticus 4:31-33 (Based On KJV)

"And he shall take away all the fat thereof, as the fat is taken away from off the offering of peace offerings; and the priest shall burn it upon the altar for a sweet savour unto the IEUE; and the priest shall make an atonement for him, and it shall be forgiven him. And if he bring a lamb for a sin offering, he shall bring it a female without blemish. And he shall lay his hand upon the head of the sin offering, and slay it for a sin offering in the place where they kill the burnt offering."

The female Lamb offerings foreshadowed the Lamb Yeshuatekani being impaled upon a stake. The fact they were female strongly suggests that the Messiah is female.

THE MESSIAH'S BREAST ARE MENTIONED IN THE SCRIPTURES

We can prove in The Messianic (New Testament) Scriptures that Yeshuatekani has breasts.

Let's look at

Luke 11:27 (Based on KJV)

"And it came to pass, as She spake these things, a certain woman of the company lifted up her voice, and said unto Her, Blessed is the womb that bare thee, and the paps which thou hast sucked."

Luke 23:29 (Based on KJV)

"For, behold, the days are coming, in the which they shall say, Blessed are the barren and the wombs that never bare, and the paps which never gave suck"

What does "paps" mean? Here's the Answer from Strong's Exhaustive Concordance pap.

From the base of massaomai; a (properly, female) breast (as if kneaded up) -- pap.

From the two Luke verses it's obvious that "paps" refers to female breasts.

"Paps" occurs three times in the Messianic Scriptures.

The third time it describes Yeshuatekani in The Scroll of Revelation and what a revelation it is.

Revelation 1:12-13 (Based on KJV)

"And I turned to see the voice that spake with me. And being turned, I saw seven golden candlesticks; And in the midst of the seven candlesticks one like unto the Descendant of Adam, clothed with a garment down to the foot, and girt about the paps with a golden girdle."

Tom Harper a scholar comments Rev 1:13: "Paps" is the archaic word for a woman's breasts. In the Greek, the word used is the plural mastos, which the lexicon defines as "the breast, esp., of the swelling breast of a woman". Rarely, the plural was used to refer to a man's breasts, but the prevailing sense is female. The fact that the figure in this passage from Revelation wore a "girdle", or cincture, about the breasts—the modern equivalent would be a brassiere—confirms that the breasts in question are female.

The Breasts here make Yeshuatekani's case for being a female much stronger.

50 OR 30 SHEKELS VALUATION FOR YESHUATEKANI

Let's look at the valuation for consecrating to IEUE.

Leviticus 27:1-7 (Based on KJV) *"Now IEUE spoke to Moses, saying, "Speak to the children of Israel, and say to them: 'When a man consecrates by a vow certain persons to IEUE, according to your valuation, if your valuation is of a male from twenty years old up to sixty years old, then your valuation shall be fifty shekels of silver, according to the shekel of the sanctuary. If it is a female, then your valuation shall be thirty shekels; and if from five years old up* to twenty years old, then your valuation for a male shall be twenty shekels, and for a female ten shekels; and if from a month old up to five years old, then your valuation for a male shall be five shekels of silver, and for a female your valuation shall be three shekels of silver; and if from sixty years old and above, if it is a male, then your valuation shall be fifteen shekels, and for a female ten shekels,"

Judas Iscariot received thirty pieces of silver as a blood money vow from the High Priest for Yeshuatekani Messiah.

This valuation was based on the valuation of a woman over twenty years and less than sixty years old consecrating them to the High Priest and Sanctuary. The valuation was 30 pieces of silver.

Mat 26:15 (KJV) "And said unto them, What will ye give me, and I will deliver him unto you? And they covenanted with him for thirty pieces of silver."

The word covenanted means "a usually formal, solemn, and binding agreement."

Mat 27:9 (KJV ADJ) "Then was fulfilled that which was spoken by Jeremy the prophet, saying, And they took the thirty pieces of silver, the price of her that was valued, whom they of the children of Israel did value."

It seems obvious that the price to turn over the Messiah to the priests was contingent on the methodology employed above.

I Am the Morning Star

We know from Revelation 22:16 that Yeshuatekani is the morning star...Psalm 22 is called **"The Doe of the Morning" or "The Doe of the Dawn"** or "The Hind of the Morning". What's a Doe? Wikipedia says "Doe is an adult female in some animal species such as deer and goat" and "A hind is a female deer, especially a red deer". Why is this important? It's important because Psalm 22 is a Psalm written by Dawid and the headings above are used in different translations.

Psalm 22 is a prophecy of the impalement of Yeshuatekani who is called "**A doe**" or "**a hind**". Both are feminine in nature. Thus the Title of Psalm 22 continues to enlightens us regarding the gender of Yeshuatekani, that being female. Here are some extracts from Psalm 22. One extract claims the "Doe" is not a man! Is this indicative of Yeshuatekani being female? Here are some extracts from Psalm 22.

To the choirmaster: according to The Doe of the Dawn. A Psalm of David.

Psalm 22 (Extracts Based on the KJV ADJ)

My El, my El, why hast thou forsaken me? why art thou so far from helping me, and from the words of my roaring?

But I am a worm, AND NO MAN; a reproach of men, and despised of the people.

All they that see me mock me: they shoot out the lip, they shake the head, saying, She trusted on IEUE that he would deliver Her: let Him deliver Her, seeing He delighted in Her.

'I am poured out like water, and all my bones are out of joint: my heart is like wax; it is melted in the midst of my bowels.....

My strength is dried up like a potsherd; and my tongue cleaveth to my jaws; and thou hast brought me into the dust of death.…..

For dogs have compassed me: the assembly of the wicked have enclosed me: they pierced my hands and my feet.….

I may tell all my bones: they look and stare upon me……

They part my garments among them, and cast lots upon my vesture…..

Had the Messiah been male wouldn't the Title of the Psalm have been "The Stag of the Morning" or "Bull of the Morning". The "and no man" suggests that the victim here is a woman. Yeshuatekani was a female impaled victim thus strengthening the female gender theory.

CHAPTER 6

Prophecies Of The Female Messiah: Yeshuatekani

THE ROSE & LILY PROPHECIES

First the rose. One of the prophecies attached to The Anointed can be found in *Isaiah 35:1-2 Based on KJV).*

The wilderness and the solitary place shall be glad for them; and the desert shall rejoice, AND BLOSSOM AS THE ROSE. It shall blossom abundantly, and rejoice even with joy and singing: the esteem of Lebanon shall be given unto it, the excellency of Carmel and Sharon, they shall see the esteem of IEUE, and the excellency of Elohim.

In this prophecy it is obvious that the blossoming of the rose refers to The Messiah. Let's confirm this by looking at commentary from the Geneva Study Bible.

The wilderness and the solitary place shall be glad for them; and the desert shall rejoice, and blossom as the rose. He (Isaiah) prophesizes of the full restoration of the Assemblies both of the Jews and Gentiles under The Messiah, which will be fully accomplished at the last day: although as yet it is compared to a desert and wilderness.

The Lilly of the Valley Messianic Prophecy

The Rose is not the only flower to symbolize The Messiah. Hosea 14 is another prophecy of The Messiah to come. Here it is in its entirety.

Israel Restored at Last - Hosea 14:5-7 (Based on KJV ADJ)

"I will be as the dew unto Israel: She shall grow as the lily, and cast forth Her roots as Lebanon. Her branches shall spread, and Her beauty shall be as the olive tree, and Her smell as Lebanon.

They that dwell under Her shadow shall return; they shall revive as the corn, and grow as the vine: the scent thereof shall be as the wine of Lebanon."

Both the Rose of Sharon and Lily of the Valley prophecies are about The Messiah returning after the end times. These prophecies are brought together in the Song of Shelemoh (Solomon).

Shir haShirim (Song of Songs) (Song of Solomon)

Judaism (from Wikipedia :) The Song was accepted into the Jewish canon of scripture in the 2nd century CE, after a period of controversy in the 1st century. It was accepted as canonical because of its supposed authorship by Shelomoh and based on an allegorical reading where the subject-matter was taken to be not sexual desire but Elohim's love for Israel.

In Judaism the man in the Song Is Our Father IEUE and the woman is Israel. (From Wikipedia) In modern Judaism, certain verses from the Song are read on Shabbat eve or at Passover to symbolize the love between the Jewish People and their Elohim.

It's enlightening that Judaism celebrates or quotes from this Song when celebrating Passover. Yeshuatekani is the Messianic Faith's Passover Lamb.

The Roman Catholic and its sister assemblies when reading the Song of Songs see the Song as an allegory of Elohim's love for His Assembly.

It is true that the male in the Song of Songs symbolizes The Father IEUE. However the female does not symbolize Israel and for the Roman Catholics and sister assemblies the female does not represent any of their assemblies.

The female in the Song of Songs symbolizes Yeshuatekani. Remember "I AM" is one of the Father's names and The Messiah's name has the Father's name in it. The prophecies symbolized by a Rose and the Lily merge together with the Father's name when the female in the Song identifies herself. She says:

Song of Shelomoh 2:1-2 (KJV)

"I am" the Rose of Sharon,
and the Lily of the valleys.
As the Lily among thorns,
so is my love among the daughters."

So the female in the Song lays claim to both The Rose Prophecy and The Lily Prophecy. Notice that the Lily is among thorns. Yeshuatekani was given a crown of thorns because She claimed to be Sovereign of the Yehudim.

Matthew 27:29 (Based on KJV)

"And when they had platted a crown of thorns, they put it upon Her head, and a reed in Her right hand: and they bowed the knee before Her, and mocked Her, saying, Hail, Sovereign of the Yehudim!"

The reason why the Jewish and Roman Catholic allegories above are invalid is because of the following verses:

Song of Shelomoh 4:7 King James Version (KJV)

"Thou art all fair, my love; there is no spot in thee."

In two other translations of the 50 or so Scriptural Translations of www.biblegateway.com we find the above translated using the words

There is no flaw or blemish on you
Every part of you is perfect

The Lady in the Song is without blemish, flawless, without a spot and is perfect. There has only been one perfect human being since The Father in Genesis in the history of peoplekind and that's Yeshuatekani.

Later on in the Song of Song's this perfection is confirmed again:

Song of Shelomoh 5:2 (KJV)

"I sleep, but my heart waketh: it is the voice of my beloved that knocketh, saying, Open to me, my sister, my love, my dove, my undefiled: for my head is filled with dew, and my locks with the drops of the night."

The translation "my perfect one" is used In 28 of the English translations available on Bible Gateway instead of undefiled and a few other translations use the word "perfect" as part of their translation.

Israel is not perfect, The Roman Catholic and sister assemblies are not perfect, only Yeshuatekani is.

Hebrews 5:8-10 King James Version (KJV)

"Though She were a Descendant yet learned She obedience by the things which She suffered; And being made perfect, She became the author of eternal deliverance unto all them that obey Her; Called of Elohim an high priest after the order of Melchisedec".

We know that Yeshuatekani is seated on the right-hand side of Our Strong One IEUE. This is confirmed twice in The Song:

Song of Shelomoh 2:6 (KJV)

"His left hand is under my head, and his right hand doth embrace me"

Song of Shelomoh 8:3 King James Version (KJV)

"His left hand should be under my head, and his right hand should embrace me."

If we would put our left hand under someone's head and then embrace them with our right hand they would have to be to the right of us.

Mark 16:19 (Based on KJV)

"So then after the Yeshuatekani had spoken unto them, She was received up into heaven, and sat on the right hand of Elohim."

The very first verse in The Messianic Scriptures tells us that Yeshuatekani was "a Son of Dawid" (David). Now Dawid didn't have a son named Yeshuatekani. It is more accurate to say Yeshuatekani was a descendant of Dawid. The Song of Songs connects The Rose of Sharon to "Dawid".

Song of Shelomoh 4:4 (Based on KJV)

"Thy neck is like the tower of Dawid builded for an armoury, whereon there hang a thousand bucklers, all shields of mighty men".

Matthew 1:1 (Based on KJV)

"The book of the generation of Yeshuatekani, the Descendant of David, the Descendant of Abraham."

Immediately after being immersed by Yohanon the Immerser the Set-Apart Spirit descended on Yeshuatekani by way of a dove.

The Set-Apart Spirit and Doves

John 1:32-33 (Based on KJV)

"And Yohanan bare record, saying, I saw the Spirit descending from heaven like a dove, and it abode upon Her. And I knew Her not: but She that sent me to immerse with water, the same said unto me, Upon whom thou shalt see the Spirit descending, and remaining on Her, the same is She which immerses with the Set-Apart Spirit."

The Song of Songs mentions "dove" six times, five in relation to The Rose of Sharon and once to Our Father. Here's one example:

Song of Shelomoh 5:2 (KJV)

"I sleep, but my heart waketh: it is the voice of my beloved that knocketh, saying, Open to me, my sister, my love, my dove, my undefiled: for my head is filled with dew, and my locks with the drops of the night."

With the dove symbolizing the Set-Apart Spirit we can connect aspects of the Messiah's life to the Song.

I Am the Good Shepherd

John 10:7-17 (Based on KJV)

"Then said Yeshuatekani unto them again, Verily, verily, I say unto you, I am the door of the sheep. All that ever came before me are thieves and robbers: but the sheep did not hear them. I am the door: by me if any person enter in, they shall be saved, and shall go in and out, and find pasture. The thief cometh not, but for to steal, and to kill, and to destroy: I am come that they might have life, and that they might have it more abundantly. I am the good shepherd: the good shepherd giveth Her life for the sheep. But he that is an hireling, and not the shepherd, whose own the sheep are not, seeth the wolf coming, and leaveth the sheep, and fleeth: and the wolf catcheth them, and scattereth the sheep. The hireling fleeth, because he is an hireling, and careth not for the sheep. I am the good shepherd, and know my sheep, and am known of mine. As the Father knoweth me, even so know I the Father: and I lay down my life for the sheep. And other sheep I have, which are not of this fold: them also I must bring, and they shall hear my voice; and there shall be one fold, and one shepherd. Therefore doth my Father love me, because I lay down my life, that I might take it again."

IEUE says the following to The Rose of Sharon.

Song of Shelomoh 4:1-2 Kings (KJV)

"Behold, thou art fair, my love; behold, thou art fair; thou hast doves' eyes within thy locks: thy hair is as a flock of goats, that appear from mount Gilead. Thy teeth are like a flock of sheep that are even shorn, which came up from the washing; whereof every one bear twins, and none is barren among them."

The Lily of the Valley's Yeshuatekani flock of sheep are perfect.

Thus a connection between Shepherd and Yeshuatekani is made.

Shepherd Keeper of the Flock

Now one of the most hidden prophecies of Yeshuatekani comes from a woman in the Pre-Messianic Scriptures.

There was a female shepherdess:

Genesis 29:1-9 King James Version (KJV)

"And he said unto them, Is he well? And they said, He is well: and, behold, Rachel his daughter cometh with the sheep. And he said, Lo, it is yet high day, neither is it time that the cattle should be gathered together: water ye the sheep, and go and feed them. And they said, We cannot, until all the flocks be gathered together, and till they roll the stone from the well's mouth; then we water the sheep. And while he yet spake with them, Rachel came with her father's sheep; for she kept them."

So very early in The Scriptures we are introduced to a female shepherdess suggesting that it is possible for The Messiah to be a Shepherdess. Now here is the hidden prophecy of Yeshuatekani to come.

Wikipedia has the answer:

Rachel (Hebrew: לְחָר, Modern Rakhél, Tiberian Rāḥēl) was the favorite of Biblical patriarch Jacob's two wives as well as the mother of Joseph and Benjamin, two of the twelve progenitors of the tribes of Israel. The name "Rachel" is from an unused root meaning: "TO JOURNEY AS AN EWE THAT IS A GOOD TRAVELER."

We know that Yeshuatekani is called a Lamb. The above can be read as follows "to journey as a female lamb that is a good traveler." The greatest traveler of all time was Our Lamb, Our Rose, Our Lily, Our Shepherd of the Sheep, Yeshuatekani.

Gold, Frankincense and Myrrh.

We find that all three gifts The Anointed received from the wise men/Magi are mentioned in connection with The Rose of Sharon and Lily of the Valley.

Matthew 2:11 (Based on KJV)

"And when they were come into the house, they saw the young child with Miryam Her mother, and fell down, and worshipped Her: and when they had opened their treasures, they presented unto Her gifts; gold, and frankincense and myrrh."

Song of Shelomoh 4:12-14 (KJV)

"A garden inclosed is my sister, my spouse; a spring shut up, a fountain sealed. Thy plants are an orchard of pomegranates, with pleasant fruits; camphire, with spikenard, Spikenard and saffron; calamus and cinnamon. with all trees of frankincense; myrrh and aloes, with all the chief spices:"

Notice that Shelomoh refers to The Rose of Sharon as sister and spouse.

Song of Shelomoh 1:10-11 (KJV)

"Thy cheeks are comely with rows of jewels, thy neck with chains of gold. We with will make thee borders of gold studs of silver".

REJECTION AND EPISODE WITH THE GUARDS

In the following verses the Messiah is rejected by the Father. Then the Rose of Sharon is beaten up and declothed.

These verses are similar to "My **El, My El,** why have you forsaken me" and other impalement events.

Shelomoh 5:2-7 (KJV)

"I sleep, but my heart waketh: it is the voice of my beloved that knocketh, saying, Open to me, my sister, my love, my dove, my undefiled: for my head is filled with dew, and my locks with the drops of the night. I have put off my coat; how shall I put it on? I have washed my feet; how shall I defile them?

My beloved put in his hand by the hole of the door, and my bowels were moved for him. I rose up to open to my beloved; and my hands dropped with myrrh, and my fingers with sweet smelling myrrh, upon the handles of the lock. I opened to my beloved; but my beloved had withdrawn himself, and was gone: my being failed when he spake: I sought him, but I could not find him; I called him, but he gave me no answer.

[My El, My El, why have you forsaken me]

"The watchmen that went about the city found me, they smote me, they wounded me; the keepers of the walls took away my veil from me."

Yeshuatekani was stripped of her clothes, crowned with thorns, beaten, spat at, mocked, stripped again and then impaled.

In the verses above The Father calls **Yeshuatekani** "my sister" showing that they are related.

Resurrection and Ascension

Song of Shelomoh 2:10-16 (KJV)

"My beloved spake, and said unto me, Rise up, my love, my fair one, and come away. For, lo, the winter is past, the rain is over and gone; The flowers appear on the earth; the time of the singing of birds is come, and the voice of the turtle is heard in our land; The fig tree putteth forth her green figs, and the vines with the tender grape give a good smell. Arise, my love, my fair one, and come away. O my dove, that art in the clefts of the rock, in the secret places of the stairs, let me see thy countenance, let me hear thy voice; for sweet is thy voice, and thy countenance is comely. Take us the foxes, the little foxes, that spoil the vines: for our vines have tender grapes. My beloved is mine, and I am his: he feedeth among the lilies.

Two celebratory RISES that can be Paired with the Resurrection and Ascension. Let's take the time to look at the Resurrection according to John.

John 20:1-17 King James Version (KJV)

"The first day of the week cometh Miryam of Magdala early, when it was yet dark, unto the sepulchre, and seeth the stone taken away from the sepulchre. Then she runneth, and cometh to Shimon Kepha

(Simon Peter), and to the other Taught One, whom Yeshuatekani loved (most likely Yohanon since Yohanon received The Scroll of Revelation), and saith unto them, They have taken away the Master out of the sepulchre, and we know not where they have laid Her.

Kepha therefore went forth, and that other Taught One, and came to the sepulchre. So they ran both together: and the other Taught One did outrun Kepha, and came first to the sepulchre.

And he stooping down, and looking in, saw the linen clothes lying; yet went he not in. Then cometh Shimon Kepha following him, and went into the sepulchre, and seeth the linen clothes lie, And the napkin, that was about Her head, not lying with the linen clothes, but wrapped together in a place by itself.

[The napkin could be used to cover her face like a veil worn by females]

Then went in also that other Taught One, which came first to the sepulchre, and he saw, and believed. For as yet they knew not the scripture, that She must rise again from the dead. Then the Taught Ones went away again unto their own home. But Miryam stood without at the sepulchre weeping: and as she wept, she stooped down, and looked into the sepulchre, And seeth two messengers in white sitting, the one at the head, and the other at the feet, where the body of Yeshuatekani had lain.

And they say unto her, Woman, why weepest thou? She saith unto them, Because they have taken away my Master, and I know not where they have laid Her. And when she had thus said, she turned herself back, and saw Yeshuatekani standing, and knew not that it was Yeshuatekani.

Yeshuatekani saith unto her, Woman, why weepest thou? whom seekest thou? She, supposing him to be the gardener, saith unto Her,

Sir, if thou have borne Her hence, tell me where thou hast laid Her, and I will take Her away. [If the Messiah were a man would she have had the strength to take a man away with her?]

Yeshuatekani saith unto her, Miryam. She turned herself, and saith unto Her, Rabboni; which is to say, Master. Yeshuatekani saith unto her, Touch me not; for I am not yet ascended to my Father: but go to my brethren, and say unto them, I ascend unto my Father, and your Father; and to my Elohim, and your Elohim."

Why did Miryam not recognize Yeshuatekani? Could it be because She was wearing a veil? Rabboni is a variation of Rabbi which means Teacher. Could it be that Rabboni is the word for a female Rabbi?

The Second Coming is called for

Song of Shelomoh 6:13 (KJV)

"Return, return, O Shulamite; return, return, that we may look upon thee. What will ye see in the Shulamite? As it were the company of two armies."

Reward for the Children

The Song of Songs describes to us that Yeshuatekani will take good care of Her children, those written in the Book of Life. (shall be spoken for)

Song of Shelomoh 8:8-10 (KJV)

"We have a little sister, and she hath no breasts: what shall we do for our sister in the day when she shall be spoken for? If she be a wall, we will build upon her a palace of silver: and if she be a door, we

will inclose her with boards of cedar. I am a wall, and my breasts like towers: then was I in his eyes as one that found favour."

I am sure I have missed some Messianic references in the Song of Songs but the evidence up to now has proven beyond a shadow of doubt that the female in the Song of Songs is the Messiah.

Who Did Yeshuatekani Love?

There are several mentions of one of the taught ones who was loved by Yeshuatekani. The taught one who was loved by Yeshuatekani also leaned on her chest. Was the loved one a romantic partner. Leaning on Yeshuatekani's chest in public is noteworthy in that it was a male leaning on Her chest a female.

(Yohanon13:23-25) *"Now there was leaning on Yeshuatekani's bosom one of his taught ones, whom Yeshuatekani loved. Shimon Kepha therefore beckoned to him, that he should ask who it should be of whom she spake. He then lying on Yeshuatekani's breast saith unto her, Master who is it?"*

In another instance we note that Yeshuatekani stands on the shore and the taught ones fail to recognize her. Is this because she is wearing a veil. When Shimon Kepha is told by the taught one who Yeshuatekani loved that Yeshuatekani was there he put on his fisherman's clothes, He was naked without his fisherman's coat and one wonders if Yeshuatekani was a male whether he would have bothered to put on his fisherman's coat.

(Yohanon 21:4) *"But when the morning was now come, Yeshuatekani stood on the shore: but the taught ones knew not that it was Yeshuatekani."*

(Yohanon 21:7) *"Therefore that taught one whom Yeshuatekani loved saith unto Kepha, It is the Master. Now when Shimon Kepha heard that it was the Master, he girt his fisher's coat unto him, (for he was naked,) and did cast himself into the sea."*

The taught one loved by Yeshuatekani was likely Yohanon. At the impalement Yohanon was given Yeshuatekani's mother to look after.

CHAPTER 7

The Wisdom Of Yeshuatekani

WISDOM IS OUR SISTER

Mat 12:42 (KJV) "The queen of the south shall rise up in the judgment with this generation, and shall condemn it: for she came from the uttermost parts of the earth to hear the wisdom of Solomon; and, behold, a greater than Solomon is here." Yeshuatekani `wisdom is greater than King Solomon. In Proverbs Wisdom is personified as a female over 50 times.

We are told that wisdom is our Sister.

Proverbs (7:1-4) "My son, keep my words, and lay up my commandments with thee. Keep my commandments, and live; and my law as the apple of thine eye. Bind them upon thy fingers, write them upon the table of thine heart. Say unto wisdom, Thou art my sister; and call understanding thy kinswoman[best friend]:"

Here's a little color on wisdom

Proverbs 4:5-13 (KJV ADJ)

"Get wisdom, get understanding: forget it not; neither decline from the words of my mouth. Forsake her not, and she shall preserve thee: love her, and she shall keep thee. Wisdom is the principal thing; therefore get wisdom: and with all thy getting get understanding. Exalt her, and she shall promote thee: she shall bring thee to honour, when thou dost embrace her. She shall give to thine head an ornament of favor: a crown of esteem shall she deliver to thee. Hear, O my son, and receive my sayings; and the years of thy life shall be many. I have taught thee in the way of wisdom; I have led thee in right paths. When thou goest, thy steps shall not be straitened; and when thou runnest thou shalt not stumble. Take fast hold of instruction; let her not go: keep her; for she is thy life."

The connection between wisdom and Yeshuatekani is extraordinary. She is our sister and we are told to keep her for she is our life.

The Throne of Elohim: IEUE & Yeshuatekani

45:6-17 (KJV ADJ) *Thy throne, O Elohim, is for ever and ever: the sceptre of thy kingdom is a right sceptre. Thou lovest righteousness, and hatest wickedness: therefore Elohim, thy Elohim, hath anointed thee with the oil of gladness above thy fellows. All thy garments smell of myrrh, and aloes, and cassia, out of the ivory palaces, whereby they have made thee glad.*

Kings' daughters were among thy honourable women: upon thy right hand did stand the queen in gold of Ophir. Hearken, O daughter, and consider, and incline thine ear; forget also thine own people, and thy father's house; So shall the king greatly desire thy beauty: for he is thy Master; and worship thou him.

And the daughter of Tyre shall be there with a gift; even the rich among the people shall intreat thy favour. The king's daughter is all esteemed within: her clothing is of wrought gold. She shall be brought unto the king in raiment of needlework: the virgins her companions that follow her shall be brought unto thee.

With gladness and rejoicing shall they be brought: they shall enter into the king's palace. Instead of thy fathers shall be thy children, whom thou mayest make princes in all the earth. I will make thy name to be remembered in all generations: therefore shall the people praise thee for ever and ever.

In this Psalm IEUE is the King and his daughter is the Queen. Yesuatekani is both daughter and Queen and sits on the right hand of the King.

Female Circumcision

Yeshuatekani was circumcised. Female circumcision was performed by Jewish people as proven by the Falashas descendants of the Israeli tribe of Dan. Yeshuatekani was a special child and needed as such to be circumcised.

Luke 2:20-22 (KJV ADJ) *And the shepherds returned, esteeming and praising Elohim for all the things that they had heard and seen, as it was told unto them. And when eight days were accomplished for the circumcising of the child, her name was called Yeshuatekani, which was so named of the messenger before she was conceived in the womb. And when the days of her purification according to the law of Moses were accomplished, they brought her to Jerusalem, to present her to IEUE;*

Falashas consider themselves descendants of the tribe of "Dan", one of the 10 "lost tribes of Israel", and were acknowledged as such, and therefore as being officially Jewish, by the Israeli government in 1975. This entitled them to the right of settling in Israel.

Ritual female genital surgery (female circumcision) is usually associated with Muslim countries although it is normative also among Ethiopian Coptic Christians. Ethiopian Jewish women immigrants to Israel report that ritual female genital surgery was normative in their culture in Ethiopia, but expressed no desire to continue the custom in Israel. Physical examination of 113 Ethiopian Jewish immigrant women in Israel found a variety of lesions in about a third of women, with 27% showing total or partial clitoral amputation. The heterogeneity of the physical findings contrasts with uniform verbal reports in interviews of having undergone a ritual of female genital surge.

So at least one of the tribes of Israel performed circumcision on females. This could have happened to Yeshuatekani.

Several arguments have been presented establishing Yeshuatekani as The Messiah. The preponderance of evidence presented should convince the reader of Yeshuatekani's gender.

CHAPTER 8

The Man Of Lawlessness

The Man of Lawlessness (A Creation of Satan)

In Second Timothy the emissary Shaul tells us "All Scripture are breathed by Elohim and profitable for teaching, for reproof, for setting straight, for instruction in righteousness, that the person of Elohim might be fitted and equipped for every good work."

In Hebrews it is written "Yeshuatekani is the same, yesterday and forever."

We can easily conclude then that Scripture is our source for determining reproof and that the Messiah kept and will keep the Ten Commandments and Torah in the future.

If we are going to point the finger at the Man of Lawlessness, we must concretely show that his beliefs are in violation of The Scriptures and his teachings to his Assembly are simply just wrong and he is guilty of committing lawlessness. The Law is headed by the Ten Commandments.

And Elohim spoke all these Words saying: I Am IEUE Thy Elohim who brought you out of the land of Egypt, out of the house of slavery.

(1) You have no other mighty elohims against my face.

(2) You do not make for yourself a carved image, or any likeness of that which is in the heavens above, or which is in the earth beneath, or which is in the waters under the earth, you do not bow down to them nor serve them. For I IEUE your Elohim am a jealous El, visiting the crookedness of the fathers on the children to the third and fourth generations of those who hate Me, but showing kindness to thousands who love me and guard My Commandments.

(3) You do not bring the Name of IEUE your Elohim to nothing, for IEUE does not leave the person unpunished who brings His Name to nothing.

(4) Remember the Sabbath Day, to Set it Apart. Six days you labor, but on the Seventh Day, is a Sabbath of IEUE your Elohim. You do not do any work, you, nor your spouse, nor your children, nor your male servants, nor your female servants, nor your cattle, nor any strangers who are within your gates. For in six days IEUE made the heavens and the earth, the sea and all that is in them and rested on the Seventh Day. Therefore IEUE blessed the Sabbath Day and Set it Apart.

(5) Respect your father and your mother so that your days are prolonged upon the earth which IEUE your Elohim is giving you.

(6) You do not murder.

(7) You do not commit adultery.

(8) You do not steal.

(9) You do not bear false witness against your neighbor.

(10) You do not covet your neighbor's house, nor your neighbor's spouse, nor their male servants, nor their female servants, nor their ox, nor their donkey, nor your neighbor's possessions.

The Prophet Daniel shares with us that in the time of the end a ruler would change the Appointed Times and the Law. The Law being the Ten Commandments and the Torah. The Appointed Times are the Sabbaths we are to keep (Daniel 7:25-27 TS).

"And it speaks words against the Most High, and it wears out the Set-Apart ones of the Most High, and it intends to change appointed times and law, and they are given into its hand for a time and times and half a time. But the Judgement shall sit, and they shall take away its rule, to cut off and to destroy, until the end. 'And the reign, and the rulership, and the greatness of the reigns under all the heavens, shall be given to the people, the Set-Apart ones of the Most High. Her reign is an everlasting reign, and all rulerships shall serve and obey Her."

We are close to the end times allowing me to look at the state of the world today to see if there is a candidate operating or ruling today that has destroyed appointed times (Sabbaths) and changed The Law. The Law being the Ten Command's and the teachings of IEUE (The Torah) and the teachings of The Messiah Yeshuatekani.

Sha'ul in his letter to Thessalonians provides us with more information on the Lawless One. He tells us that the Lawless One is according to the working of Satan.

Thus THE CREATION OF SATAN. (2 THE 2:1-10 TS)

'As to the coming of our Master The Messiah Yeshuatekani and our gathering together to Her, we ask you, bretheren, not to become easily unsettled in mind or troubled, either by spirit or by word or by letter, as if from us, as if the day of IEUE has come. Let no one deceive you in any way, because the falling away(Movement away from true worship) is to come first, and the man of lawlessness is to be revealed, the son of destruction, who opposes and exalts himself above all that is called Elohim's or that is worshipped, so that he sits as Elohim in the Dwelling Place of Elohim, showing himself that he is Elohim. Do you not remember that I told you this while I was still with you? And now you know what restrains, for him to be revealed in his time. For the secret of lawlessness is already at work – only until he who now restrains comes out of the midst. And then the lawless one shall be revealed, whom the Master shall consume with the Spirit of Her mouth and bring to naught with the manifestation of Her coming. The coming of the lawless one is according to the working of Satan, with all power and signs and wonders of falsehood, and with all deceit of unrighteousness in those perishing, because they did not receive the love of the truth, in order for them to be saved.'

The Man of Lawlessness is the pope. He is responsible for the catechism and all actions pertaining to past popes. The Man of Lawlessness prevents us from receiving the love of the truth. What follows will be many truths substantiated with Scripture identifying him without a shadow of any doubt. The Roman Catholic First Commandment contains the Second Commandment.

"(2) You do not make for yourself a carved image, or any likeness of that which is in the heavens above, or which is in the earth beneath, or which is in the waters under the earth, you do not bow down to them nor serve them. For I IEUE your Elohim am a jealous El, visiting the crookedness of the fathers on the children to the third and fourth generations of those who hate Me, but showing kindness to thousands who love me and guard My Commandments.

Vatican 1st Commandment

"You shall have no other gods before me. You shall not make for yourself an idol, whether in the form of anything that is in heaven above, or that is on the earth beneath, or that is in the water under the earth. You shall not bow down to them or worship them; for I the

Lord your God am a jealous God, punishing children for the iniquity of parents, to the third and the fourth generation of those who reject me, but showing steadfast love to the thousandth generation of those who love me and keep my commandments.

It is often the case that the second portion of the Commandment is left out of printed materials. Here is the Vatican Commandments. As you can see the First Commandment leaves out the idol prohibition and punishment associated with idol worship.

Abbreviated Catholic Ten Commandments

1) I, the Lord, am your God. You shall not have other gods besides me.

2) You shall not take the name of the Lord God in vain

3) Remember to keep holy the Lord's Day

4) Honor your father and your mother

5) You shall not kill

6) You shall not commit adultery

7) You shall not steal

8) You shall not bear false witness

9) You shall not covet your neighbor's wife

10) You shall not covet your neighbor's goods

The Vatican led by the pope does not enforce it allowing statues of Jesus, Miryam and the Saints facilitating kneeling and Praying to the statues. This constitutes idolatry and worship. The Vatican calls it "reverence" of the statue which is against Scripture *(Matthew 22:37 Adjusted KJV) Yeshuatekani said unto him, Thou shalt love*

IEUE thy Elohim with all thy heart, and with all thy spirit, and with all thy mind.

We cannot love or worship IEUE with all our strength, spirit and heart if we are busy praying to a Jesus or Miryam (Miryam) Statue. In conclusion at the very least the Roman Catholic Church fails to enforce or teach their first Commandment and this constitutes a break of the Commandment affecting millions and millions of the Roman Catholic faithful.

Breaking The Sabbath Commandment

First let's look at IEUE's Sabbath instructions. *(Exodus 31:13 Adjusted KJV) Speak thou also unto the children of Israel, saying, Verily my sabbaths ye shall keep: for it is a sign between me and you throughout your generations; that ye may know that I am IEUE that doth set you apart.*

Keeping the Sabbaths is a sign between IEUE and ourselves, It sets us apart from the rest of the world and it's for all generations. Furthermore (Exodus 31:16 states that Sabbath keeping is a perpetual covenant.

We are to keep The Sabbaths and Festivals in order to be signed by IEUE to be set-apart as one of his people.

Here is the Sabbath Commandment again: "Remember the Sabbath Day, to Set it Apart. Six days you labor, but on the Seventh Day, is a Sabbath of IEUE your Elohim. You do not do any work, you, nor your spouse, nor your children, nor your male servants, nor your female servants, nor your cattle, nor any strangers who are within your gates. For in six days IEUE made the heavens and the earth, the sea and all that is in them and rested on the Seventh Day. Therefore IEUE blessed the Sabbath Day and Set it Apart."

The Sabbath is the seventh day of the week. Roman Catholics and other Christian Denominations treat the Sabbath as Sunday the first day of the week.

The LORD'S Day is a major change to the Sabbath of IEUE. Around 336 CE at the Council of Laodicea the Sabbath was moved to the Day of the Unconquered Sun which is Sunday. This trampling of the Fourth Commandment and Covenant with IEUE is a sin every Sunday Christian person is going to be judged on.

The Vatican Church even admits to changing the Sabbath Commandment.

2190 The sabbath which represented the completion of the first creation has been replaced by Sunday which recalls the new creation inaugurated by the Resurrection of Christ.

No person or pope has the authority to change what IEUE inscribed on the Ten Commandment Tablets and no person or pope has the authority to change a Covenant that is for every generation including ours. Included in the Sabbaths of IEUE are the following Sabbaths.

Weekly Sabbath

Day of the New Moon Sabbath

Passover

Feast of Unleavened Bread

Feast of First Fruits

Feast of the Set-Apart Spirit (Pentecost)

Feast of Trumpets

Day of Atonement

The Eighth Day

Roman Catholicism does not celebrate any of the Festivals of IEUE. They celebrate Christmas, Easter, Good Friday and Palm Sunday and Christmas is a lie, Yeshuatekani was born in the Spring or Fall. Santa Claus does not exist and many if not all of the Christmas traditions are sourced in pagan festivals of the past.

Easter: During pagan times a dawn goddess of fertility Eostre was celebrated in a festival. Eostre is a female goddess and the foundation of Easter. Is this because Yeshuatekani is a female, Thus the merger of a pagan festival and Christianity suggests the Messiah is female.

The Christian Sunday Sabbath made by men around the 4th century has not been blessed and Set-apart by the Father IEUE. There is no mention of the Sabbath being changed in The Bible. There will be a time when the Sabbath will be celebrated worldwide on the seventh day. Isaiah 66:23 "And it shall come to pass, that from one new moon to another, and from one sabbath to another, shall all flesh come to worship before me, saith IEUE."

The Master of the Sabbath is Yeshuatekani and She will be the Master of ceremonies beginning with Her return to earth. She will not be doing this on the Christian Sabbath. Why then are we celebrating Sunday's when it is obvious from the Bible that the Sabbath Day should be the 7th day of the week. Worshiping the Sabbath Day on Sundays is a sin and violates the Sabbath Commandment.

Hebrews 13:8 Yeshuatekani Messiah is the same yesterday, and today, and forever. Malachi 3:6 For I am IEUE, I change not; ……. The Messiah won't change to Christian Sabbaths and IEUE doesn't change and he won't rest on the First Day of the Week-Sunday. Sunday worship is a betrayal of responsibility and. a slap in the faces of IEUE and Yeshuatekani Messiah.

Priests, Reverends, Pastors are deceiving their assemblies keeping them from the truth and will be held accountable for their treachery.

With the partial merger of the First and Second Commandment a need for another Commandment to make ten commandments was required. The Vatican took the tenth Commandment and made two commandments out of it.

Vatican 9th Commandment "You shall not covet your neighbor's wife."

Vatican 10th Commandment "You shall not covet your neighbor's goods."

Actual 10th Commandment. You do not covet your neighbor's house, nor your neighbor's spouse, nor their male servants, nor their female servants, nor their ox, nor their donkey, nor your neighbor's possessions.

Nobody Is to be Called Father

Pope comes from "Papa" which means Father. All priests are called "Father". This is despite not having legitimate children. Now if Yeshuatekani gave you instructions would you not follow them. As the Mother Church would you not be incented to follow Yeshuatekani's orders. Here they are:

Matthew 23:7-9 (Adjusted KJV)

"And greetings in the markets, and to be called of men, Rabbi, Rabbi. But be not ye called Rabbi: for one is your Master, even Messiah; and all ye are brethren. And call no man your father upon the earth: for one is your Father, which is in heaven."

The Roman Catholic Church will provide excuses for using "Father" but the fact remains they are in violation of Scripture. By calling themselves "Father" they are putting themselves on the same plain level as Elohim. This is an abomination to IEUE and Yeshuatekani.

The pope is also known as "The Vicar of Christ". Vicar means "instead of" or "in place of" so not only does the pope call himself Father but he is here instead of the Messiah. The Messiah was tortured, beaten and impaled and yet the pope claims to be Messiah on earth.

What it Takes to be a Bishop

Pope Francis is also called the Bishop of Rome. He is celibate, has no wife and has no children that we know of. He has a number of celibate Bishops from all over the world reporting to him. Here are the credentials needed to be a Bishop in the Roman Catholic Church.

Bishops are always men. In addition, Canon 378 §1 requires that a candidate for the episcopacy should be: outstanding in solid faith, good morals, piety, zeal for souls, wisdom, prudence, human virtues, and endowed with other qualities which make him suitable to fulfill the office in question; of good reputation; at least thirty-five years old; ordained to the presbyterate for at least five years; In possession of a doctorate or at least a licentiate in sacred scripture, theology, or canon law from an institute of higher studies approved by the Apostolic See, or at least truly expert in the same disciplines.

A bishop (English derivation from the New Testament Greek ἐπίσκοπος, epískopos, "overseer", "guardian") is an ordained or consecrated member of the Christian clergy who is generally entrusted with a position of authority and oversight. Bishop means overseer and The Scriptures tell us what the qualifications are to be a Bishop or Overseer.

1 Timothy 3:3-7 (Adjusted KJV)

"This is a true saying, if a man desire the office of a bishop, he desireth a good work. A bishop then must be blameless, the husband of one wife, vigilant, sober, of good behaviour, given to hospitality, apt to teach; Not given to wine, no striker, not greedy of filthy lucre; but patient, not a brawler, not covetous; One that ruleth well his own house, having his children in subjection with all gravity;

(For if a man know not how to rule his own house, how shall he take care of the assembly of IEUE?) Not a novice, lest being lifted up with pride he fall into the condemnation of the devil. Moreover he must have a good report of them which are without; lest he fall into reproach and the snare of the devil."

The priesthood is celibate without any wives or children. This is a clear violation of Scripture.

Amazingly enough the pope is infallible. In Roman Catholic theology, the doctrine that the pope, acting as supreme teacher and under certain conditions, cannot err when he teaches in matters of faith or morals. Being called 'infallible', means any of the following.

Some (or all) statements or teachings made by the pope can be relied on to be certainly true.

The pope always makes good and moral choices, and his actions may never be considered immoral or evil.

The pope is always right, and never wrong or incorrect.

Romans 3:23 (KJV Adjusted) *"For all have sinned, and come short of the esteem of Elohim".*

1 John 1:8 *"If we say that we have no sin, we deceive ourselves, and the truth is not in us."*.

The pope should not be called infallible which implies perfection. The pope sins every time he administers Sunday Mass.

CHAPTER 9

The Restoration Of The Truth

Purgatory

Dave Hunt in his book "A Women Rides the Beast" writes the following on Purgatory:

"Catholicism teaches that while Christ's death made it possible for sins to be forgiven, the pardoned sinner must himself suffer undefined pain or torment of unknown intensity and duration to be purged and thereby made fit for heaven......"

The word purgatory does not appear in the Bible. Furthermore,

1 John 1:7 (Adjusted KJV) *'But if we walk in the light, as she is in the light, we have fellowship one with another, and the blood of Yeshuatekani Messiah his daughter cleanseth us from all sin.'*

1 John 1:9 (Adjusted KJV) *"If we confess our sins, she is faithful and just to forgive us our sins, and to cleanse us from all unrighteousness."*

Bottom line is Yeshuatekani Messiah cleanses us from sin, there is no need to pass through the fires of a non-existent purgatory.

Queen of Heaven

In 1954, four years after the dogma of the Assumption was declared, Pope Pius XII established the Feast of the Queenship of Miryam. On August 22, the Roman Catholic Church celebrates a memorial in honor of the Queenship of Miryam. This memorial is placed an octave, that is, eight days after celebrating Miryam's Assumption into Heaven. The Queenship can be considered a prolongation of the celebration of the Assumption. Our Blessed Mother leads her children to the Sacred Heart of her Son, and Our Lady of Perpetual Help is the patron of St. John Neumann's order, the Redemptorists. With great confidence in her intercession, we entrust all of our families to the powerful prayers and protection of the Queen of Heaven, "Regina Coeli" (Latin for Queen of Heaven.)

Messiah has a problem with all this Miryam worship. Messiah Yeshuatekani is Queen of Heaven and Miryam Dogmas are food for the dragon.

Miryam has many titles in the Roman Catholic Church including Mother of God, Queen of Heaven, Virgin and others, The beloved Miryam is worshipped worldwide. There are thousands of shrines dedicated to her and just more than a handful to Jesus Christ. When did Miryam die? Why is there no mention of her assumption to heaven in the Book of Revelation. Surely such an event would merit writing something about. The Bible is silent on the issue. Anyway all of this Miryam than Queen of Heaven talk is moot, The Queen of Heaven is Yeshuatekani.

Apparitions of Miryam

A Marian apparition is a supernatural appearance by the Blessed Virgin Miryam. The figure is often named after the town where it is reported, or on the sobriquet given to Miryam on the occasion of the apparition. They have been interpreted in religious terms as theophanies.

The effect on the Roman Catholic Church has been staggering.

The conversion of millions of people to Roman Catholicism.

The construction of some of the largest Roman Catholic Marian churches ever.

The formation of the largest Marian Movements and Societies ever.

The spread of Marian devotions (such as the rosary) to millions of people.

The declaration of specific Marian dogmas and doctrines.

Hundreds of millions of Marian pilgrimages.

The devotion/worship of Jesus and Miryam has taken Roman Catholics away from the truth. We are supposed to love The Father IEUE with all our strength. IEUE was so fed up with Roman Catholics loving Miryam that he sent a delusion to help Roman Catholics believe in her. Since Roman Catholics don't search for the truth Father IEUE sends a delusion to the earth in the way of Marian Apparitions to encourage false worship.

2 Thessalonians 2:10-12 (Adjusted KJV) *"And with all deceivableness of unrighteousness in them that perish; because they received not the love of the truth, that they might be saved. And for this cause Elohim shall send them a strong delusion, that they should believe a lie: That they all might be damned who believed not the truth, but had pleasure in unrighteousness."*

What is the delusion? Apparitions of Miryam is IEUE's delusion. The whole Mariology idolatry experience is an exercise in pleasurable unrighteousness that results in damnation. The Kneeling down and making prayers to a statue is an act of idolatry.

Transubstantiation

(Wikipedia) Transubstantiation is, according to the teachings of the Roman Catholic Church, the change of substance or essence by which the bread and wine offered in the sacrifice of the sacrament of the Eucharist during the Mass, become, in reality, the body and blood of Jesus Christ.......The manner in which the change occurs, the Roman Catholic Church teaches, is a mystery: "The signs of bread and wine become, in a way surpassing understanding, the Body and Blood of Christ."

There are over a billion Roman Catholics, and let's use 500.000.000 as an estimate of those receiving communion. That's a lot of "Body" and "" and would take multiple Jesus's to supply that enormous load and then he would have to regenerate himself so parishioners can in the following week be cannibals again.

The process of changing bread and wine into a body and blood is termed a mystery, meaning magic has to take place. The priest plays sorcerer and transforms a wafer and red wine into the body and blood of Jesus Christ. Well there is news for sorcerers and it goes something like this;

***Revelation 21:8 (KJV)** But the fearful, and unbelieving, and the abominable, and murderers, and whoremongers, and sorcerers, and idolaters, and all liars, shall have their part in the lake which burneth with fire and brimstone: which is the second death.*

Transubstantiation is a Roman Catholic Tradition; it is completely anti-scriptural. The Roman Catholic Church is guilty of lying to its parishioners. The wafer/host and wine remain unchanged after the priests magic touch. So when the priest says "Body of Christ" to the gullible parishioner he is lying and breaking a Commandment. Scripturally we should have none of that:

Mark 7:8-9 (Adjusted KJV) *For laying aside the commandment of Elohim, ye hold the tradition of men, as the washing of pots and cups: and many other such like things ye do. And he said unto them, Full well ye reject the commandment of Elohim, that ye may keep your own tradition.*

Communion is the highlight of the Mass and it includes sorcery and a lie both of which result in a trip to the Lake of Fire.

Prayer

Yeshuatekani gave the following prayer instructions:

Matthew 6:13 (Adjusted KJV)

"But thou, when thou prayest, enter into thy closet, and when thou hast shut thy door, pray to thy Father which is in secret; and thy Father which seeth in secret shall reward thee openly.

But when ye pray, use not vain repetitions, as the heathen do: for they think that they shall be heard for their much speaking. Be not ye therefore like unto them: for your Father knoweth what things ye have need of, before ye ask him."

After this manner therefore pray ye: Our Father which art in heaven, Set-Apart be thy name. Thy kingdom come, Thy will be done in earth, as it is in heaven. Give us this day our daily bread and forgive us our debts, as we forgive our debtors. And lead us not into temptation, but deliver us from evil: For thine is the kingdom, and the power, and the esteem, forever. Amen."

And a little more from Mark 11:24-26 (KJV)

"Therefore I say unto you, What things soever ye desire, when ye pray, believe that ye receive them, and ye shall have them. And when ye stand praying, forgive, if ye have ought against any: that your Father also which is in heaven may forgive you your trespasses. But if ye do not forgive, neither will your Father which is in heaven forgive your trespasses."

Yeshuatekani gives us a prayer outline for us to build our prayer around. She directs us to pray to the Father. Prayer is a very personal communication with our Father IEUE. If the Father is accepting all prayers, why is it that the Roman Catholic Church encourages prayers to Miryam and the Saints? Praying to Miryam is **unscriptural** as is praying to the Saints.

Babbling Rosary

The Rosary is a series of prayers where at its heart it repeats ten Hail Miryam Prayers for each Mystery. Each Mystery has a group of five meditations. Each Mystery generates 50 Hail Miryam's.

Each Hail Miryam is a simple 2 or 3 lined prayer. There are 53 prayer for 1 Mystery, 103 for 2 Mysteries, 153 for 3, 203 for 4 and 253 for 5.

Let's put this in context….if ½ the number of Catholics (600,000) complete a 2 Mystery Prayer of 103 Hail Miryam's per day then Mother Miryam would have to hear 61.8 Million Hail Miryam's a day. These are vain repetitions and we are expressly taught to avoid them by The Messiah Yeshuatekani.

The Rosary is not supported by Scripture and is dominated by vain repetitions. We are to love our Father IEUE with all our heart. Praying to Miryam is idolatry because it takes love and respect away from The Father. What does the Father IEUE think about the Rosary? According to the Second Commandment He is jealous of our idolatry. He is jealous of all those prayers. He wants us all to direct our prayers to Him.

I have illustrated multiple ways the Roman Catholic Church is anti-Scriptural and is engaged in Non-Messianic practices or traditions. Additionally Rome has replaced the Jewish Calendar with the Gregorian Calendar. More importantly Rome has changed the Jewish or Messianic Calendar to a Sunday based system. The man in charge of all these "discretions" and "traditions" is the pope. The pope is the "Man of Lawlessness".

Mark of the Beast

Rev 18:4 (KJV) *"And I heard another voice from heaven saying, Come out of her, my people, that ye be not partakers of her sins, and that ye receive not of her plagues,"*

The Come out of her my people refers to the end time Beast that opposes IEUE. The "my People" already have a relationship with IEUE but have been deceived by the Beast to worship in opposition to IEUE.

Rev 20:4 (KJV Adj) *"And I saw thrones, and they sat upon them, and judgment was given unto them: and I saw the spirits of them that were beheaded for the witness of Yeshuatekani, and for the word of Elohim, and which had not worshipped the beast, neither his image, neither had received his mark upon their foreheads, or in their hands; and they lived and reigned with Messiah a thousand years."*

So it's a great thing not to be tagged with Mark of the Beast. What is the Mark Of The Beast? Let's start with the Mark of IEUE. Another translation for "mark" in Strong's Concordance is "sign".

Exodus 31:13 (KJV ADJ) *"Speak thou also unto the children of Israel, saying, Verily my sabbaths ye shall keep: for it is a sign between me and you throughout your generations; that ye may know that I am IEUE that I am setting you apart.*

The sign is between us and Elohim and it denotes keeping of the Sabbath. The sign/mark of the Beast is keeping the Sunday Sabbath. The Beast Leader is the Man of Lawlessness the pope. The Beast is Sunday Christianity.

Revelation 13:16-17 (KJV) *"And he causeth all, both small and great, rich and poor, free and bond, to receive a mark in their right hand, or in their foreheads: And that no man might buy or sell, save he that had the mark, or the name of the beast, or the number of his name"*

The forehead represents the mind (Hebrews 10:16). A person will be marked in the forehead by a decision to keep Sunday as a Set-Apart day. The hand is a symbol of work (Ecclesiastes 9:10). A person will be marked in the hand by working on Elohim's Set-Apart Sabbath or by going along with Sunday laws for practical reasons (job, family, etc.). The sign, or mark, for either Elohim or the beast will be invisible to people. You will, in essence, mark yourself by accepting either Elohim's mark—the Sabbath—or the beast's mark—Sunday. Though invisible to men, Elohim will know who has which mark (2 Timothy 2:19).

If you are a Sunday Christian worshipper you have been marked and you can buy or sell on the Jewish Sabbath.

The Appointed Sabbaths and Feasts of IEUE

Leviticus 23 outlines nine appointed feasts including the Sabbath.

The Weekly Sabbath [Exo 31:12-17 KJV Adj]

And IEUE spake unto Moses, saying, Speak thou also unto the children of Israel, saying, Verily my Sabbaths ye shall keep: for it is a sign between me and you throughout your generations; that ye may know that I am IEUE that doth set you apart.

Ye shall keep the Sabbath therefore; for it is set-apart unto you: every one that defileth it shall surely be put to death: for whosoever doeth any work therein, they shall be cut off from among his people.

Six days may work be done; but in the seventh is the Sabbath of rest, Set-Apart to IEUE: whosoever doeth any work in the Sabbath day, he shall surely be put to death. Wherefore the children of Israel shall keep the Sabbath, to observe the Sabbath throughout their generations, for a perpetual covenant.

It is a sign between me and the children of Israel for ever: for in six days IEUE made heaven and earth, and on the seventh day he rested, and was refreshed.

Each of the Appointed Feasts has a linkage to The Messiah, either "Fulfilled" or "Foreshadowing" events to come.

Yeshuatekani is "Master of the Sabbath (Mat 12:8, Adj KJV)". She also is the High **Priest (Heb 4:14)** and as such will in the future be Master of Sabbath ceremonies worshipping the Father.

(Isa 66:23 Adj KJV) "And it shall come to pass, that from one new moon to another, and from one sabbath to another, shall all flesh come to worship before me, saith IEUE"

The New Moon Sabbath is not defined in Scriptures. However Scriptures inclusive of New Moon indicate it to be a day similar to a weekly Sabbath. It is obvious that this is a day to celebrate the first day of the month.

1 Chronicles 23:31 *"And to offer all burnt sacrifices unto IEUE in the sabbaths, in the new moons, and on the set feasts, by number, according to the order commanded unto them, continually before IEUE"*

Celebration of the Sabbath is preceded by a preparation day so one can assume celebration of the New Moon Sabbath Day is also is preceded by a preparation day.

The eight feasts or days the Father IEUE calls for us to observe are:

Passover

Feast of Unleavened Bread

Feast of First Fruits

Feast of Weeks

Feast of Trumpets

Day of Atonement

Feast of Booths

The Eighth Day

PASSOVER

The origin of Passover is when IEUE promised to redeem His people from the bondage of Egypt. When Pharaoh refused, IEUE sent ten plagues to Egypt. The tenth and worst of the plagues was the death of all the firstborn in Egypt.

The night of the first Passover was the night of the tenth plague. On that fateful night, IEUE instructed the Israelites to make an offering of a spotless lamb and mark their doorposts and lintels with its blood. Then, when IEUE passed through the nation, He would "pass over" the households that had the sheep's blood on their doors. At midnight the Messenger of Death killed the first born of Egyptian families resulting in Pharoah setting the Israelites free.

Passover is a remembrance of IEUE's redemption.

The Passover Lamb was also a foreshadow of the Messiah's impalement. She was killed at Passover after attending a Passover meal (The Last Supper). Her blood shed on the stake provides us with a chance at eternal life as her blood represents forgiveness and payment for sins. By (spiritually) applying Her blood to our lives by faith, we trust Yeshuatekani to save us from death.

Feast of Unleavened Bread

The Feast of Unleavened Bread pointed to the Messiah's sinless life (as leaven is a picture of sin in The Scriptures), making Her the perfect offering for our sins. Yeshuatekani's body was in the grave during the first days of this feast, like a kernel of wheat planted and waiting to burst forth as the bread of life.

Unleavened bread is a symbol of Passover. Leaven represents sin. Matzah stands for "without sin" portraying Yeshuatekani as the only human being without sin. Yeshuatekani said that the "bread of Elohim" is She who comes down from heaven and gives life to the world" and that She (Yeshuatekani) is the "Bread of life," the "bread that came from heaven, "the living bread" which a person may eat and not die (John 6:32, 35, 41,48). While leaven is a symbol of sin, the Messiah is "unleavened" or sinless. She conquers the grave with her resurrection because she is not a sinner under the curse of death. Yeshuatekani was scourged and pierced at Her Impalement. The only type of bread eaten during Feast of Unleavened Bread is made with flour and water only and it is striped and pierced during baking.

The Messianic Fulfillment is redemption through the impalement.

Feast of First Fruits

The priests offered Passover lambs on the 14th day of the month of Nisan, and the first day of Passover was the 15th. The Feast of First Fruits was celebrated the third day, the 16th of Nisan. This "third day" celebration was the same day that Yeshuatekani resurrected from the dead. In 1 Corinthians 15:20 Paul refers to Yeshuatekani the first fruits of the dead. She represents the first of the great harvest of spirits — including you — that will resurrect to eternal life because of the new covenant in their blood (Luke 22:20).

First Fruits is a picture of Yesuatekeni's resurrection. That event gave new meaning to this agricultural holiday. The taught one Paul, a Jewish believer and Rabbi wrote, "but Messiah has indeed been raised from the dead, the first fruits who have fallen asleep. For since death came through, the resurrection of the dead comes also through a person' For as in Adam all die, so in Messiah all will be made alive. But each in turn: Messiah, the first fruits; then when she comes those that belong to her.

The Messianic Fulfillment was the resurrection of Yeshuatekani.

Feast of Pentecost (Weeks)

Pentecost marks the coming of the Set-Apart Spirit among the taught ones and followers of Yeshuatekani.

The events of the day are foretold Yeshuatekani in the first chapter of the Acts of the Apostles, just before her Ascension. While her followers were with the risen Messiah, she tells them, "John baptized with water, but you will be baptized with the Set-Apart Spirit not many days from now" (Acts 1:5, NRSV). She goes on to say to them, "You will receive power when the Set-Apart Spirit has come upon you; and you will be my witnesses in Jerusalem, in all Judea and Samaria, and to the ends of the earth" (Acts 1:8).

The followers would not wait long for the promised Set-Apart Spirit. The author of Acts, traditionally believed to be written by Luke, recounts:

"When the day of Pentecost had come, they were all together in one place. And suddenly from heaven there came a sound like the rush of a violent wind, and it filled the entire house where they were sitting. Divided tongues, as of fire, appeared among them, and a tongue rested on each of them. All of them were filled with the Set-Apart Spirit and began to speak in other languages, as the Spirit gave them ability. Now there were devout Jews from every nation under heaven living in Jerusalem. And at this sound the crowd gathered and was bewildered, because each one heard them speaking in the native language of each" (Acts 2:1-6).

We celebrate Pentecost as the inauguration of the Assemblies mission in the world. Empowered by the gift of the Set-Apart Spirit, we are to go out into our neighborhoods and the wider world—to Jerusalem, to Judea and Samaria, and to the ends of the earth—witnessing to the risen Messiah.

The Messianic fulfillment is the birth of the Messianic Assembly and coming of the Set-Apart Spirit.

Feast of Trumpets

The Ten Days of Repentance begins with Rosh Hashanah (Feast of Trumpets) on the first day and Yom Kippur (Day of Atonement) the last day. This 10-day period is also called "The Days of Awe".

Jewish tradition says that Elohim writes every persons words, deeds and thoughts in the Book of Life which he opens and examines on this day. If good deeds outnumber sinful ones for the past year, that person's name will be inscribed in the book for another year on Yom Kippur.

So during the Feast Of Trumpets (Rosh Hashanah) through the Ten Days of Repentance, people can repent of their sins and do good deeds to increase their chances of being inscribed in the Book of Life.

In the Scroll of Revelation Seven messengers sound their trumpets one by one. This will be a time of horror and judgment upon the earth that will be unmatched by any other time in human history. It will all be completed by the end of May 2028.

The Messianic Fulfillment is the Last Trumpet blown in the Book of Revelation signaling the return of Yeshuatekani Messiah.

Day of Atonement (Yom Kippur)

The Day of Atonement is a yearly feast instituted by Elohim to completely cover (pay the penalty) for all the sins of the people of Israel. When the Temple in Jerusalem was destroyed in 70 AD, the Jewish people could no longer present the required offerings on the Day of Atonement, so it came to be observed as a day of repentance, self-denial, charitable works, prayer, and fasting.

No work is performed on Yom Kippur. Two goats were elected for the grand ceremony, the high priest would place his hands on the head of the live goat and confess the sins of the whole nation before the altar of burnt offering. The first goat would be offered for the sins of the people and then he would give the live goat to an appointed person who carried it outside the camp and set it free into the wilderness. Symbolically, the **"scapegoat"** would carry away the sins of the people.

Today, the ten days between Rosh Hashanah and Yom Kippur are days of repentance, when Jews express remorse for their sins through prayer and fasting. Yom Kippur is the final day of judgment when each person's fate is sealed by IEUE for the upcoming year.

Jewish tradition tells how IEUE opens the Book of Life and studies the words, actions, and thoughts of every person whose name he has written there. If a person's good deeds outweigh or outnumber their sinful acts, his or her name will remain inscribed in the book for another year.

The blood offering for the sins of Israel pointed to Yeshuatekani being the blood offering for the people and the goat carrying the sins of Israel into the wilderness was called the Azazel goat. Azazel is a demonic entity. The sins of the goat are carried out to the wilderness. For Christians today, Yeshuatekani took all our sins, sending them far away. The Jewish people, however, didn't have this amazing gift during their time. Therefore, the goat took the weight of their sins.

The Day of Atonement differs from the other festivals because Elohim commands His people to fast (not eat or drink) on this day to draw close to Him. All the other festivals involve enjoying food and drink.

Removing food and drink on this day reminds us that man cannot live by food and water alone, but needs Elohim, who is the creator and sustainer of all things. Atonement also pictures the reconciliation of mankind to Elohim, made possible by the offering of Yeshuatekani Messiah.

The Messianic fulfillment will be Yeshuatekani holding Azazel Goat (Satan) accountable for all the sins by putting him out in the wilderness in the Lake of Fire.

The Feast of Tabernacles,

(aka The Feast of Booths or Sukkot)

Sukkot represents the final harvest when all nations will share in the joy and blessings of Elohim's Sovereigndom.

Zechariah 14:16-19 (KJV)

"And it shall come to pass, that every one that is left of all the nations which came against Jerusalem shall even go up from year to year to worship the Queen, the Master of hosts, and to keep the feast of tabernacles. And it shall be, that who so will not come up of all the families of the earth unto Jerusalem to worship the Queen, the Master of hosts, even upon them shall be no rain. And if the family of Egypt go not up, and come not, that have no rain; there shall be the plague, wherewith the Master will smite the heathen that come not up to keep the feast of tabernacles. This shall be the punishment of Egypt, and the punishment of all nations that come not up to keep the feast of tabernacles."

The Feast reminds us of the wandering in the desert. For forty years the people wandered living in tents and booths. The Feast also marks the final harvest making it a joyful harvest celebration together with it being a memorial of tabernacles in the wilderness.

The Messianic fulfillment will have all the nations of the world come to worship the Queen with those nations that refuse receiving plagues.

The Eighth Day

The Eighth Day is a solemn gathering immediately after the Festival of Booths.

This is a reach. In Catholicism Octave means an eight-day celebration, that is, the prolongation of a feast to the eighth day (dies octava) inclusive. The feast itself is considered the first day, and it is followed by six days called "days within the octave." The eighth or octave day is kept with greater solemnity than the "days within the octave."

The Easter Octave is from Easter Sunday to the Second Sunday of Easter or Divine Mercy Sunday, each day being another "little Easter." The Easter octave "overrides" any other feasts on the calendar. Christmas also has an octave, but it is very different from Easter, because it is filled with various feast days, but yet each day is still another "little Christmas."

It is also said that Jesus rose from the dead on the eighth day (which is why Sundays are considered on par with solemnities). So Sunday is the Eighth Day.

The Messianic Fulfillment is The Judgment where we are judged. The Catholic participants in the Eighth Day will be punished severely.

All of the above are the Appointed festivals and are found in Leviticus 23.

The exception is the New Moon Sabbath which we should assume is a Sabbath for the new month. It is preceded by a Preparation Day.

Hanukkah & Purin

There are two Feasts not found in the appointed Feasts of Leviticus 23; They are the Feast Of Dedication aka Hanukkah and the Feast of Lots aka Purim. The Feast of Dedication commemorates the purification of the temple which occurred in 165 BC as the Maccabees victory over the Greeks. The Greek King Antiochus Epiphanes had previously defiled the Palace (Temple) by sacrificing a pig on the alter and covering the Scripture Scrolls with pigs blood.

Hanukkah aka Feast of Lights because of a legendary miraculous provision of oil for the eternal light in the palace. After cleansing the palace the supply of oil to relight the eternal flame (the symbol of Elohim's presence) was enough for one day. Elohim performed a great miracle and the flame burned for the eight days necessary to purify oil.

Hanukkah also called the Festival of Lights is primary a family celebration that centers around lighting nine candles. One candle is lit each on the candle stick holder called a menorah, Each night a new candle is placed on the menorah until all nine candles are lit.

The Feast of Lots aka Purim is a celebration of Elohim's faithfulness, deliverance, and protection. Although the Jews were sentenced to death by King Xerxes' original decree, through Queen Esther's courageous intervention and willingness to face death, the people's lives were spared. Similarly, all of us who have sinned have been issued a decree of death, but through the intervention of Yeshuatekani Messiah, the Messiah, the old decree has been satisfied and a new proclamation of eternal life has been established.

Romans 6:23

For the wages of sin is death, but the free gift of Elohim is eternal life through Messiah Yeshuatekani our Master (NLT).

Appointments of IEUE

And IEUE spake unto Mosheh, saying,

2 Speak unto the children of Israel, and say unto them, Concerning the feasts of the IEUE, which ye shall proclaim to be a Set-Apart gathering, even these are my feasts.

Sabbath

3 Six days shall work be done: but the seventh day is the sabbath of rest, a Set-Apart gathering; ye shall do no work therein: it is the sabbath of IEUE in all your dwellings.

4 These are the feasts of IEUE; even Set-Apart gatherings which ye shall proclaim in their seasons.

Passover

5 In the fourteenth day of the first month at even is the IEUE passover.

Festival of Unleavened Bread

6 And on the fifteenth day of the same month is the feast of unleavened bread unto IEUE seven days ye must eat unleavened bread.

7 In the first day ye shall have a Set-Apart gathering: ye shall do no servile work therein.

8 But ye shall offer an offering made by fire unto IEUE seven days: in the seventh day is a Set-Apart gathering: ye shall do no servile work therein.

9 And IEUE spake unto Mosheh, saying,

Day of First Fruits

10 Speak unto the children of Israel, and say unto them, When ye be come into the land which I give unto you, and shall reap the harvest thereof, then ye shall bring a sheaf of the firstfruits of your harvest unto the priest:

11 And he shall wave the sheaf before, to be accepted for you: on the morrow after the sabbath the priest shall wave it.

12 And ye shall offer that day when ye wave the sheaf an he lamb without blemish of the first year for a burnt offering unto the IEUE.

13 And the meat offering thereof shall be two tenth deals of fine flour mingled with oil, an offering made by fire unto the IEUE for a sweet savour: and the drink offering thereof shall be of wine, the fourth part of an hin.

14 And ye shall eat neither bread, nor parched corn, nor green ears, until the selfsame day that ye have brought an offering unto your Elohim: it shall be a statute forever throughout your generations in all your dwellings.

Festival of Weeks (Pentecost)

15 And ye shall count unto you from the morrow after the sabbath, from the day that ye brought the sheaf of the wave offering; seven sabbaths shall be complete:

16 Even unto the morrow after the seventh sabbath shall ye number fifty days; and ye shall offer a new meat offering unto the IEUE. [Count 7 Sabbaths then count 50 days}

17 Ye shall bring out of your habitations two wave loaves of two tenth deals; they shall be of fine flour; they shall be baken with leaven; they are the firstfruits unto IEUE..

18 And ye shall offer with the bread seven lambs without blemish of the first year, and one young bullock, and two rams: they shall be for a burnt offering unto IEUE, with their meat offering, and their drink offerings, even an offering made by fire, of sweet savour unto IEUE.

19 Then ye shall offer one kid of the goats for a sin offering, and two lambs of the first year for an offering of peace offerings.

20 And the priest shall wave them with the bread of the firstfruits for a wave offering before the IEUE with the two lambs: they shall be Set-Apart to IEUE for the priest.

21 And ye shall proclaim on the selfsame day, that it may be a Set-Apart gathering unto you: ye shall do no servile work therein: it shall be a statute forever in all your dwellings throughout your generations.

22 And when ye reap the harvest of your land, thou shalt not make clean riddance of the corners of thy field when thou reapest, neither shalt thou gather any gleaning of thy harvest: thou shalt leave them unto the poor, and to the stranger: I am IEUE your Elohim

The Feast of Trumpets

23 And IEUE spake, saying,

24 Speak unto the children of Israel, saying, In the seventh month, in the first day unto Moshehof the month, shall ye have a sabbath, a memorial of blowing of trumpets, a Set-Apart gathering.

25 Ye shall do no servile work therein: but ye shall offer an offering made by fire unto IEUE.

The Day of Atonement

26 And IEUE spake unto Mosheh, saying,

27 Also on the tenth day of this seventh month there shall be a day of atonement: it shall be a Set-Apart gathering unto you; and ye shall afflict your beings and offer an offering made by fire unto IEUE.

28 And ye shall do no work in that same day: for it is a day of atonement, to make an atonement for you before IEUE your Elohim.

29 For whatsoever being it be that shall not be afflicted in that same day, he shall be cut off from among his people.

30 And whatsoever being it be that doeth any work in that same day, the same being l will I destroy from among his people.

31 Ye shall do no manner of work: it shall be a statute for ever throughout your generations in all your dwellings.

32 It shall be unto you a sabbath of rest, and ye shall afflict your beings: in the ninth day of the month at even, from even unto even, shall ye celebrate your sabbath.

Feast of Tabernacles/Booths

33 And IEUE spake unto Mosheh, saying,

34 Speak unto the children of Israel, saying, The fifteenth day of this seventh month shall be the feast of tabernacles for seven days unto IEUE.

35 On the first day shall be a Set-Apart gathering ye shall do no servile work therein.

Eighth Day

36 Seven days ye shall offer an offering made by fire unto IEUE: on the eighth day shall be Set-Apart gathering unto you; and ye shall offer an offering made by fire unto IEUE is a solemn assembly; and ye shall do no servile work therein.

37 These are the feasts of IEUE, which ye shall proclaim to be Set-Apart gatherings, to offer an offering made by fire unto the IEUE, a burnt offering, and a meat offering, a sacrifice, and drink offerings, every thing upon his day:

38 Beside the sabbaths of IEUE, and beside your gifts, and beside all your vows, and beside all your freewill offerings, which ye give unto IEUE.

39 Also in the fifteenth day of the seventh month, when ye have gathered in the fruit of the land, ye shall keep a feast unto IEUE seven days: on the first day shall be a sabbath, and on the eighth day shall be a sabbath.

40 And ye shall take you on the first day the boughs of goodly trees, branches of palm trees, and the boughs of thick trees, and willows of the brook; and ye shall rejoice before IEUE your Elohim seven days.

41 And ye shall keep it a feast unto IEUE seven days in the year. It shall be a statute for ever in your generations: ye shall celebrate it in the seventh month.

42 Ye shall dwell in booths seven days; all that are Israelites born shall dwell in booths:

43 That your generations may know that I made the children of Israel to dwell in booths, when I brought them out of the land of Egypt: I am IEUE your Elohim.

44 And Mosheh declared unto the children of Israel the feasts of IEUE.

King James Version (ADJ KJV).

CHAPTER 10

Building The Calendar

Calendar begins with the first New Moon after the Spring Equinox (March 20). The New Moon is dark for a couple of days and when it reaches >= 5% illumination (assume New Moon sighted) then a preparation day is set followed by the New Moon Celebration.

New Moon Celebration based on % Illumination

New Moon	0.70% Dark	4.20%	10.40% Moon Sighted	Prep Day	New Moon Celebration
08-Apr-24	09-Apr	10-Apr	11-Apr	12-Apr	13-Apr-24

Starting point for the new calendar is the first celebration of the new moon after the Spring Equinox. Which was 13 April 2024. The First New Moon Celebration equals the first day of the year.

The New Moon Celebration also sets off the timing for the regular Sabbath. The Sabbath is 7 days after the New Moon and continues its seven day intervals until The following New Year's New Moon.

Layer into the calendar the appointments according to IEUE's instructions. Calculate monthly the New Moon Celebration and add to calendar. The data source for moon information is timeanddate.com/moon/Israel/Jerusalem.

I changed the month named "Tammuz" because it is derived from the Goddess Tammuz. I changed the name to "Roset". Giving any credit to a God or Goddess is a violation of the first commandment.

Here are the appointment Days with Instructions

Weekly Sabbath - No work and Assembly

New Moon Sabbath - No work and Assembly

Passover – Eat meal at evening – between sunset and nightfall.

Festival of Unleavened Bread – Eat no food with yeast in it. Eat Unleavened bread. On the First and Seventh Day are no Servile Work days (Heavy Manual labor) and Assembly days.

Feast of Weeks (Pentecost) – Assembly and no Servile Work.

Feast of Trumpets – Blowing of Trumpets, Assembly and no Servile Work

Day of Atonement – Assembly, no Servile Work and full day fast.

Feast of Booths – First Day Assembly, no Servile Work

Eighth Day – Assembly and No Servile Work.

NEXT STEPS

Embrace Yeshuatekani as our Messiah and IEUE as our Father.

Stop attending churches whose Sabbath is on Sunday's. Stop giving them money. We no longer wish to support the upkeep of Sunday based churches.

The Second Commandment states that we do not create items of idolatry and worship or serve them. Throw away or destroy statues of Jesus, Myriam and the Saints. Throw away or destroy pictures of Jesus, Myriam and the Saints. Throw away rosary beads and start praying to IEUE alone.

Avoid Christmas, Easter and other Christian holidays.

Keep the Ten Commandments

Start Assemblies of family and friends. Assign somebody to be Pastor.

APPENDIX

Nostradamus Pope Prophecy.

Nostradamus was a French reputed seer who published collections of prophecies that have since become widely famous. The prophecies called quatrains were written in ten centuries of 100 quatrains, The tenth century has forty-two quatrains. One of the quatrains includes the pope and the Rose.

Century II Quatrain 97

> Roman Pontiff beware of approaching
>
> The City that two rivers flow through
>
> Near there your blood will come to spurt
>
> You and yours when the Rose will flourish

The city of Roman is crossed by two rivers: the Tiber, which runs from East to West, and the river L'Aniene which runs from Northeast to North. Within the city it runs into the Tiber.

Roman Pontiff is the pope and he will spill is blood when the Rose (Yeshuatekani) flourishes.

THE TEN COMMANDMENTS

And Elohim spoke all these Words saying: I Am IEUE Thy Elohim who brought you out of the land of Egypt, out of the house of slavery.

(1) You have no other mighty elohims against my face.

(2) You do not make for yourself a carved image, or any likeness of that which is in the heavens above, or which is in the earth beneath, or which is in the waters under the earth, you do not bow down to them nor serve them. For I IEUE your Elohim am a jealous El, visiting the crookedness of the fathers on the children to the third and fourth generations of those who hate Me, but showing kindness to thousands who love me and guard My Commandments.

(3) You do not bring the Name of IEUE your Elohim to nothing, for IEUE does not leave the person unpunished who brings His Name to nothing

(4) Remember the Sabbath Day, to Set it Apart. Six days you labor, but on the Seventh Day, is a Sabbath of IEUE your Elohim. You do not do any work, you, nor your spouse, nor your children, nor your male servants, nor your female servants, nor your cattle, nor any strangers who are within your gates. For in six days IEUE made the heavens and the earth, the sea and all that is in them and rested on the Seventh Day. Therefore IEUE blessed the Sabbath Day and Set it Apart.

(5) Respect your father and your mother so that your days are prolonged upon the earth which IEUE your Elohim is giving you.

(6) You do not murder.

(7) You do not commit adultery.

(8) You do not steal.

(9) You do not bear false witness against your neighbor.

(10) You do not covet your neighbor's house, nor your neighbor's spouse, nor their male servants, nor their female servants, nor their ox, nor their donkey, nor your neighbor's possessions

SABBATH AND APPOINTMENT CALENDAR

First New Moon Sabbath after Spring Equinox is beginning of year

Spring Equinox was Mar 20-h.

Date			Day	Month
01-Jan-25			28	Kislev
02-Jan-25			29	Kislev
03-Jan-25			30	Kislev
04-Jan-25		New Month Sabbath	1	Tevet
05-Jan-25			2	Tevet
06-Jan-25			3	Tevet
07-Jan-25			4	Tevet
08-Jan-25			5	Tevet
09-Jan-25			6	Tevet
10-Jan-25			7	Tevet
11-Jan-25		Sabbath	8	Tevet
12-Jan-25			9	Tevet
13-Jan-25			10	Tevet
14-Jan-25			11	Tevet
15-Jan-25			12	Tevet
16-Jan-25			13	Tevet
17-Jan-25			14	Tevet
18-Jan-25		Sabbath	15	Tevet

19-Jan-25		16	Tevet
20-Jan-25		17	Tevet
21-Jan-25		18	Tevet
22-Jan-25		19	Tevet
23-Jan-25		20	Tevet
24-Jan-25		21	Tevet
25-Jan-25	Sabbath	22	Tevet
26-Jan-25		23	Tevet
27-Jan-25		24	Tevet
28-Jan-25		25	Tevet
29-Jan-25		26	Tevet
30-Jan-25		27	Tevet
31-Jan-25		28	Tevet
01-Feb-25	Sabbath	29	Tevet
02-Feb-25	New Moon Sabbath	1	Shevat
03-Feb-25		2	Shevat
04-Feb-25		3	Shevat
05-Feb-25		4	Shevat
06-Feb-25		5	Shevat
07-Feb-25		6	Shevat
08-Feb-25	Sabbath	7	Shevat
09-Feb-25		8	Shevat
10-Feb-25		9	Shevat
11-Feb-25		10	Shevat
12-Feb-25		11	Shevat
13-Feb-25		12	Shevat
14-Feb-25		13	Shevat
15-Feb-25	Sabbath	14	Shevat
16-Feb-25		15	Shevat
17-Feb-25		16	Shevat
18-Feb-25		17	Shevat
19-Feb-25		18	Shevat

Date	Event	Day	Month
20-Feb-25		19	Shevat
21-Feb-25		20	Shevat
22-Feb-25	Sabbath	21	Shevat
23-Feb-25		22	Shevat
24-Feb-25		23	Shevat
25-Feb-25		24	Shevat
26-Feb-25		25	Shevat
27-Feb-25		26	Shevat
28-Feb-25		27	Shevat
01-Mar-25	Sabbath	28	Shevat
02-Mar-25		29	Shevat
03-Mar-25		30	Shevat
04-Mar-25	New Moon Sabbath	1	Adar 1
05-Mar-25		2	Adar 1
06-Mar-25		3	Adar 1
07-Mar-25		4	Adar 1
08-Mar-25	Sabbath	5	Adar 1
09-Mar-25		6	Adar 1
10-Mar-25		7	Adar 1
11-Mar-25		8	Adar 1
12-Mar-25		9	Adar 1
13-Mar-25		10	Adar 1
14-Mar-25		11	Adar 1
15-Mar-25	Sabbath	12	Adar 1
16-Mar-25		13	Adar 1
17-Mar-25	Purim	14	Adar 1
18-Mar-25		15	Adar 1
19-Mar-25		16	Adar 1
20-Mar-25		17	Adar 1
21-Mar-25		18	Adar 1
22-Mar-25	Sabbath	19	Adar 1
23-Mar-25		20	Adar 1

24-Mar-25			21	Adar 1
25-Mar-25			22	Adar 1
26-Mar-25			23	Adar 1
27-Mar-25			24	Adar 1
28-Mar-25			25	Adar 1
29-Mar-25		Sabbath	26	Adar 1
30-Mar-25			27	Adar 1
31-Mar-25			28	Adar 1
01-Apr-25			29	Adar 1
02-Apr-25		New Moon New Year Sabbath Reset Sabbath	1	Nisan
03-Apr-25			2	Nisan
04-Apr-25			3	Nisan
05-Apr-25			4	Nisan
06-Apr-25			5	Nisan
07-Apr-25			6	Nisan
08-Apr-25			7	Nisan
09-Apr-25		Sabbath	8	Nisan
10-Apr-25			9	Nisan
11-Apr-25			10	Nisan
12-Apr-25			11	Nisan
13-Apr-25			12	Nisan
14-Apr-25			13	Nisan
15-Apr-25		Passover	14	Nisan
16-Apr-25		1st Day of Unleavened Bread	15	Nisan
17-Apr-25		Day of First Fruits	16	Nisan
18-Apr-25		3rd Day of Unleavened Bread	17	Nisan
19-Apr-25		4th Day of Unleavened Bread	18	Nisan
20-Apr-25		5th Day of Unleavened Bread	19	Nisan
21-Apr-25		6th Day of Unleavened Bread	20	Nisan
22-Apr-25		7th Day of Unleavened Bread	21	Nisan
23-Apr-25	1	Sabbath	22	Nisan

Date	#		Day	#	Month
24-Apr-25				23	Nisan
25-Apr-25				24	Nisan
26-Apr-25				25	Nisan
27-Apr-25				26	Nisan
28-Apr-25				27	Nisan
29-Apr-25				28	Nisan
30-Apr-25	2		Sabbath	29	Nisan
01-May-25				30	Nisan
02-May-25			New Moon Sabbath	1	Iyar
03-May-25				2	Iyar
04-May-25				3	Iyar
05-May-25				4	Iyar
06-May-25				5	Iyar
07-May-25	3		Sabbath	6	Iyar
08-May-25				7	Iyar
09-May-25				8	Iyar
10-May-25				9	Iyar
11-May-25				10	Iyar
12-May-25				11	Iyar
13-May-25				12	Iyar
14-May-25	4		Sabbath	13	Iyar
15-May-25				14	Iyar
16-May-25				15	Iyar
17-May-25				16	Iyar
18-May-25				17	Iyar
19-May-25				18	Iyar
20-May-25				19	Iyar
21-May-25	5		Sabbath	20	Iyar
22-May-25				21	Iyar
23-May-25				22	Iyar
24-May-25				23	Iyar
25-May-25				24	Iyar

26-May-25			25	Iyar
27-May-25			26	Iyar
28-May-25	6	Sabbath	27	Iyar
29-May-25			28	Iyar
30-May-25			29	Iyar
31-May-25		New Moon Sabbath	1	Sivan
01-Jun-25			2	Sivan
02-Jun-25			3	Sivan
03-Jun-25			4	Sivan
04-Jun-25	7	Sabbath	5	Sivan
05-Jun-25	1		6	Sivan
06-Jun-25	2		7	Sivan
07-Jun-25	3		8	Sivan
08-Jun-25	4		9	Sivan
09-Jun-25	5		10	Sivan
10-Jun-25	6		11	Sivan
11-Jun-25	7	Sabbath	12	Sivan
12-Jun-25	8		13	Sivan
13-Jun-25	9		14	Sivan
14-Jun-25	10		15	Sivan
15-Jun-25	11		16	Sivan
16-Jun-25	12		17	Sivan
17-Jun-25	13		18	Sivan
18-Jun-25	14	Sabbath	19	Sivan
19-Jun-25	15		20	Sivan
20-Jun-25	16		21	Sivan
21-Jun-25	17		22	Sivan
22-Jun-25	18		23	Sivan
23-Jun-25	19		24	Sivan
24-Jun-25	20		25	Sivan
25-Jun-25	21	Sabbath	26	Sivan
26-Jun-25	22		27	Sivan

27-Jun-25	23		28	Sivan
28-Jun-25	24		29	Sivan
29-Jun-25	25	New Moon Sabbath	1	Rose
30-Jun-25	26		2	Rose
01-Jul-25	27		3	Rose
02-Jul-25	28	Sabbath	4	Rose
03-Jul-25	29		5	Rose
04-Jul-25	30		6	Rose
05-Jul-25	31		7	Rose
06-Jul-25	32		8	Rose
07-Jul-25	33		9	Rose
08-Jul-25	34		10	Rose
09-Jul-25	35	Sabbath	11	Rose
10-Jul-25	36		12	Rose
11-Jul-25	37		13	Rose
12-Jul-25	38		14	Rose
13-Jul-25	39		15	Rose
14-Jul-25	40		16	Rose
15-Jul-25	41		17	Rose
16-Jul-25	42	Sabbath	18	Rose
17-Jul-25	43		19	Rose
18-Jul-25	44		20	Rose
19-Jul-25	45		21	Rose
20-Jul-25	46		22	Rose
21-Jul-25	47		23	Rose
22-Jul-25	48		24	Rose
23-Jul-25	49	Sabbath	25	Rose
24-Jul-25	50		26	Rose
25-Jul-25		Feast of Weeks	27	Rose
26-Jul-25			28	Rose
27-Jul-25			29	Rose
28-Jul-25			30	Rose

Date		Event	Day	Month
29-Jul-25		New Moon Sabbath	1	Av
30-Jul-25		Sabbath	2	Av
31-Jul-25			3	Av
01-Aug-25			4	Av
02-Aug-25			5	Av
03-Aug-25			6	Av
04-Aug-25			7	Av
05-Aug-25			8	Av
06-Aug-25		Sabbath	9	Av
07-Aug-25			10	Av
08-Aug-25			11	Av
09-Aug-25			12	Av
10-Aug-25			13	Av
11-Aug-25			14	Av
12-Aug-25			15	Av
13-Aug-25		Sabbath	16	Av
14-Aug-25			17	Av
15-Aug-25			18	Av
16-Aug-25			19	Av
17-Aug-25			20	Av
18-Aug-25			21	Av
19-Aug-25			22	Av
20-Aug-25		Sabbath	23	Av
21-Aug-25			24	Av
22-Aug-25			25	Av
23-Aug-25			26	Av
24-Aug-25			27	Av
25-Aug-25			28	Av
26-Aug-25			29	Av
27-Aug-25		New Moon Sabbath	1	Elul
28-Aug-25			2	Elul
29-Aug-25			3	Elul

30-Aug-25		4	Elul
31-Aug-25		5	Elul
01-Sep-25		6	Elul
02-Sep-25		7	Elul
03-Sep-25	Sabbath	8	Elul
04-Sep-25		9	Elul
05-Sep-25		10	Elul
06-Sep-25		11	Elul
07-Sep-25		12	Elul
08-Sep-25		13	Elul
09-Sep-25		14	Elul
10-Sep-25	Sabbath	15	Elul
11-Sep-25		16	Elul
12-Sep-25		17	Elul
13-Sep-25		18	Elul
14-Sep-25		19	Elul
15-Sep-25		20	Elul
16-Sep-25		21	Elul
17-Sep-25	Sabbath	22	Elul
18-Sep-25		23	Elul
19-Sep-25		24	Elul
20-Sep-25		25	Elul
21-Sep-25		26	Elul
22-Sep-25		27	Elul
23-Sep-25		28	Elul
24-Sep-25	Sabbath	29	Elul
25-Sep-25		30	Elul
26-Sep-25	Feast of Trumpets	1	Tishrei
27-Sep-25		2	Tishrei
28-Sep-25		3	Tishrei
29-Sep-25		4	Tishrei
30-Sep-25		5	Tishrei

01-Oct-25		Sabbath	6	Tishrei
02-Oct-25			7	Tishrei
03-Oct-25			8	Tishrei
04-Oct-25			9	Tishrei
05-Oct-25		Day of Atonement	10	Tishrei
06-Oct-25			11	Tishrei
07-Oct-25			12	Tishrei
08-Oct-25		Sabbath	13	Tishrei
09-Oct-25			14	Tishrei
10-Oct-25		1st Day of Feast of Booths	15	Tishrei
11-Oct-25		2nd Day of Feast of Booths	16	Tishrei
12-Oct-25		3rd Day of Feast of Booths	17	Tishrei
13-Oct-25		4th Day of Feast of Booths	18	Tishrei
14-Oct-25		5th Day of Feast of Booths	19	Tishrei
15-Oct-25		`6th Day of FOB/Sabbath	20	Tishrei
16-Oct-25		7th Day of Feast of Booths	21	Tishrei
17-Oct-25		Eighth Day	22	Tishrei
18-Oct-25			23	Tishrei
19-Oct-25			24	Tishrei
20-Oct-25			25	Tishrei
21-Oct-25			26	Tishrei
22-Oct-25		Sabbath	27	Tishrei
23-Oct-25			28	Tishrei
24-Oct-25			29	Tishrei
25-Oct-25			30	Tishrei
26-Oct-25		New Moon Sabbath	1	Cheshvan
27-Oct-25			2	Cheshvan
28-Oct-25			3	Cheshvan
29-Oct-25		Sabbath	4	Cheshvan
30-Oct-25			5	Cheshvan
31-Oct-25			6	Cheshvan
01-Nov-25			7	Cheshvan

Date		Event	Day	Month
02-Nov-25			8	Cheshvan
03-Nov-25			9	Cheshvan
04-Nov-25			10	Cheshvan
05-Nov-25		Sabbath	11	Cheshvan
06-Nov-25			12	Cheshvan
07-Nov-25			13	Cheshvan
08-Nov-25			14	Cheshvan
09-Nov-25			15	Cheshvan
10-Nov-25			16	Cheshvan
11-Nov-25			17	Cheshvan
12-Nov-25		Sabbath	18	Cheshvan
13-Nov-25			19	Cheshvan
14-Nov-25			20	Cheshvan
15-Nov-25			21	Cheshvan
16-Nov-25			22	Cheshvan
17-Nov-25			23	Cheshvan
18-Nov-25			24	Cheshvan
19-Nov-25		Sabbath	25	Cheshvan
20-Nov-25			26	Cheshvan
21-Nov-25			27	Cheshvan
22-Nov-25			28	Cheshvan
23-Nov-25			29	Cheshvan
24-Nov-25			30	Cheshvan
25-Nov-25		New Moon Sabbath	1	Kislev
26-Nov-25		Sabbath	2	Kislev
27-Nov-25			3	Kislev
28-Nov-25			4	Kislev
29-Nov-25			5	Kislev
30-Nov-25			6	Kislev
01-Dec-25			7	Kislev
02-Dec-25			8	Kislev
03-Dec-25		Sabbath	9	Kislev

Date			Day	Month
04-Dec-25			10	Kislev
05-Dec-25			11	Kislev
06-Dec-25			12	Kislev
07-Dec-25			13	Kislev
08-Dec-25			14	Kislev
09-Dec-25			15	Kislev
10-Dec-25		Sabbath	16	Kislev
11-Dec-25			17	Kislev
12-Dec-25			18	Kislev
13-Dec-25			19	Kislev
14-Dec-25			20	Kislev
15-Dec-25			21	Kislev
16-Dec-25			22	Kislev
17-Dec-25		Sabbath	23	Kislev
18-Dec-25			24	Kislev
19-Dec-25		Hanukkah Begins Lasts 8 Days	25	Kislev
20-Dec-25			26	Kislev
21-Dec-25			27	Kislev
22-Dec-25			28	Kislev
23-Dec-25			29	Kislev
24-Dec-25		New Moon Sabbath	1	Tevet
25-Dec-25			2	Tevet
26-Dec-25			3	Tevet
27-Dec-25			4	Tevet
28-Dec-25			5	Tevet
29-Dec-25			6	Tevet
30-Dec-25			7	Tevet
31-Dec-25		Sabbath	8	Tevet
01-Jan-26			9	Tevet
02-Jan-26			10	Tevet
03-Jan-26			11	Tevet
04-Jan-26			12	Tevet

Date		Day	Month
05-Jan-26		13	Tevet
06-Jan-26		14	Tevet
07-Jan-26	Sabbath	15	Tevet
08-Jan-26		16	Tevet
09-Jan-26		17	Tevet
10-Jan-26		18	Tevet
11-Jan-26		19	Tevet
12-Jan-26		20	Tevet
13-Jan-26		21	Tevet
14-Jan-26	Sabbath	22	Tevet
15-Jan-26		23	Tevet
16-Jan-26		24	Tevet
17-Jan-26		25	Tevet
18-Jan-26		26	Tevet
19-Jan-26		27	Tevet
20-Jan-26		28	Tevet
21-Jan-26	Sabbath	29	Tevet
22-Jan-26		30	Tevet
23-Jan-26	New Moon Sabbath	1	Shevat
24-Jan-26		2	Shevat
25-Jan-26		3	Shevat
26-Jan-26		4	Shevat
27-Jan-26		5	Shevat
28-Jan-26	Sabbath	6	Shevat
29-Jan-26		7	Shevat
30-Jan-26		8	Shevat
31-Jan-26		9	Shevat
01-Feb-26		10	Shevat
02-Feb-26		11	Shevat
03-Feb-26		12	Shevat
04-Feb-26	Sabbath	13	Shevat
05-Feb-26		14	Shevat

06-Feb-26		15	Shevat
07-Feb-26		16	Shevat
08-Feb-26		17	Shevat
09-Feb-26		18	Shevat
10-Feb-26		19	Shevat
11-Feb-26	Sabbath	20	Shevat
12-Feb-26		21	Shevat
13-Feb-26		22	Shevat
14-Feb-26		23	Shevat
15-Feb-26		24	Shevat
16-Feb-26		25	Shevat
17-Feb-26		26	Shevat
18-Feb-26	Sabbath	27	Shevat
19-Feb-26		28	Shevat
20-Feb-26		29	Shevat
21-Feb-26		30	Shevat
22-Feb-26	New Moon Sabbath	1	Adar
23-Feb-26		2	Adar
24-Feb-26		3	Adar
25-Feb-26	Sabbath	4	Adar
26-Feb-26		5	Adar
27-Feb-26		6	Adar
28-Feb-26		7	Adar
01-Mar-26		8	Adar
02-Mar-26		9	Adar
03-Mar-26		10	Adar
04-Mar-26	Sabbath	11	Adar
05-Mar-26		12	Adar
06-Mar-26		13	Adar
07-Mar-26	Purim	14	Adar
08-Mar-26		15	Adar
09-Mar-26		16	Adar

10-Mar-26		17	Adar
11-Mar-26	Sabbath	18	Adar
12-Mar-26		19	Adar
13-Mar-26		20	Adar
14-Mar-26		21	Adar
15-Mar-26		22	Adar
16-Mar-26		23	Adar
17-Mar-26		24	Adar
18-Mar-26	Sabbath	25	Adar
19-Mar-26		26	Adar
20-Mar-26		27	Adar
21-Mar-26		28	Adar
22-Mar-26		29	Adar
23-Mar-26	New Year New Month Reset Sabbath	1	Nisan
24-Mar-26		2	Nisan
25-Mar-26		3	Nisan
26-Mar-26		4	Nisan
27-Mar-26		5	Nisan
28-Mar-26		6	Nisan
29-Mar-26		7	Nisan
30-Mar-26	Sabbath	8	Nisan
31-Mar-26		9	Nisan
01-Apr-26		10	Nisan
02-Apr-26		11	Nisan
03-Apr-26		12	Nisan
04-Apr-26		13	Nisan
05-Apr-26	Passover	14	Nisan
06-Apr-26	1st Day of Unleavened Bread	15	Nisan
07-Apr-26	Day of First Fruits	16	Nisan
08-Apr-26	3rd Day of Unleavened Bread	17	Nisan
09-Apr-26	4th Day of Unleavened Bread	18	Nisan
10-Apr-26	5th Day of Unleavened Bread	19	Nisan

Date	#	Event	Day	Month
11-Apr-26		6th Day of Unleavened Bread	20	Nisan
12-Apr-26		7th Day of Unleavened Bread	21	Nisan
13-Apr-26	1	Sabbath	22	Nisan
14-Apr-26			23	Nisan
15-Apr-26			24	Nisan
16-Apr-26			25	Nisan
17-Apr-26			26	Nisan
18-Apr-26			27	Nisan
19-Apr-26			28	Nisan
20-Apr-26	2	Sabbath	29	Nisan
21-Apr-26		New Moon Sabbath	1	Iyar
22-Apr-26			2	Iyar
23-Apr-26			3	Iyar
24-Apr-26			4	Iyar
25-Apr-26			5	Iyar
26-Apr-26			6	Iyar
27-Apr-26	3	Sabbath	7	Iyar
28-Apr-26			8	Iyar
29-Apr-26			9	Iyar
30-Apr-26			10	Iyar
01-May-26			11	Iyar
02-May-26			12	Iyar
03-May-26			13	Iyar
04-May-26	4	Sabbath	14	Iyar
05-May-26			15	Iyar
06-May-26			16	Iyar
07-May-26			17	Iyar
08-May-26			18	Iyar
09-May-26			19	Iyar
10-May-26			20	Iyar
11-May-26	5	Sabbath	21	Iyar
12-May-26			22	Iyar

13-May-26			23	Iyar
14-May-26			24	Iyar
15-May-26			25	Iyar
16-May-26			26	Iyar
17-May-26			27	Iyar
18-May-26	6	Sabbath	28	Iyar
19-May-26			29	Iyar
20-May-26			30	Iyar
21-May-26		New Moon Sabbath	1	Sivan
22-May-26			2	Sivan
23-May-26			3	Sivan
24-May-26			4	Sivan
25-May-26	7	Sabbath	5	Sivan
26-May-26	1		6	Sivan
27-May-26	2		7	Sivan
28-May-26	3		8	Sivan
29-May-26	4		9	Sivan
30-May-26	5		10	Sivan
31-May-26	6		11	Sivan
01-Jun-26	7	Sabbath	12	Sivan
02-Jun-26	8		13	Sivan
03-Jun-26	9		14	Sivan
04-Jun-26	4		15	Sivan
05-Jun-26	10		16	Sivan
06-Jun-26	11		17	Sivan
07-Jun-26	12		18	Sivan
08-Jun-26	13	Sabbath	19	Sivan
09-Jun-26	14		20	Sivan
10-Jun-26	15		21	Sivan
11-Jun-26	16		22	Sivan
12-Jun-26	17		23	Sivan
13-Jun-26	18		24	Sivan

14-Jun-26	19		25	Sivan
15-Jun-26	20	Sabbath	26	Sivan
16-Jun-26	21		27	Sivan
17-Jun-26	22		28	Sivan
18-Jun-26	23		29	Sivan
19-Jun-26	24	New Moon Sabbath	1	Rose
20-Jun-26	25		2	Rose
21-Jun-26	26		3	Rose
22-Jun-26	27	Sabbath	4	Rose
23-Jun-26	28		5	Rose
24-Jun-26	29		6	Rose
25-Jun-26	30		7	Rose
26-Jun-26	31		8	Rose
27-Jun-26	32		9	Rose
28-Jun-26	33		10	Rose
29-Jun-26	34	Sabbath	11	Rose
30-Jun-26	35		12	Rose
01-Jul-26	36		13	Rose
02-Jul-26	37		14	Rose
03-Jul-26	38		15	Rose
04-Jul-26	39		16	Rose
05-Jul-26	40		17	Rose
06-Jul-26	41	Sabbath	18	Rose
07-Jul-26	42		19	Rose
08-Jul-26	43		20	Rose
09-Jul-26	44		21	Rose
10-Jul-26	45		22	Rose
11-Jul-26	46		23	Rose
12-Jul-26	47		24	Rose
13-Jul-26	48	Sabbath	25	Rose
14-Jul-26	49		26	Rose
15-Jul-26	50	.	27	Rose

16-Jul-26	Feast of Weeks	28	Rose
17-Jul-26		29	Rose
18-Jul-26	New Moon Sabbath	1	Av
19-Jul-26		2	Av
20-Jul-26	Sabbath	3	Av
21-Jul-26		4	Av
22-Jul-26		5	Av
23-Jul-26		6	Av
24-Jul-26		7	Av
25-Jul-26		8	Av
26-Jul-26		9	Av
27-Jul-26	Sabbath	10	Av
28-Jul-26		11	Av
29-Jul-26		12	Av
30-Jul-26		13	Av
31-Jul-26		14	Av
01-Aug-26		15	Av
02-Aug-26		16	Av
03-Aug-26	Sabbath	17	Av
04-Aug-26		18	Av
05-Aug-26		19	Av
06-Aug-26		20	Av
07-Aug-26		21	Av
08-Aug-26		22	Av
09-Aug-26		23	Av
10-Aug-26	Sabbath	24	Av
11-Aug-26		25	Av
12-Aug-26		26	Av
13-Aug-26		27	Av
14-Aug-26		28	Av
15-Aug-26		29	Av
16-Aug-26		30	Av

17-Aug-26	New Moon Sabbath	1	Elul
18-Aug-26		2	Elul
19-Aug-26		3	Elul
20-Aug-26		4	Elul
21-Aug-26		5	Elul
22-Aug-26		6	Elul
23-Aug-26		7	Elul
24-Aug-26	Sabbath	8	Elul
25-Aug-26		9	Elul
26-Aug-26		10	Elul
27-Aug-26		11	Elul
28-Aug-26		12	Elul
29-Aug-26		13	Elul
30-Aug-26		14	Elul
31-Aug-26	Sabbath	15	Elul
01-Sep-26		16	Elul
02-Sep-26		17	Elul
03-Sep-26		18	Elul
04-Sep-26		19	Elul
05-Sep-26		20	Elul
06-Sep-26		21	Elul
07-Sep-26	Sabbath	22	Elul
08-Sep-26		23	Elul
09-Sep-26		24	Elul
10-Sep-26		25	Elul
11-Sep-26		26	Elul
12-Sep-26		27	Elul
13-Sep-26		28	Elul
14-Sep-26	Sabbath	29	Elul
15-Sep-26	Feast of Trumpets	1	Tishrei
16-Sep-26		2	Tishrei
17-Sep-26		3	Tishrei

18-Sep-26		4	Tishrei
19-Sep-26		5	Tishrei
20-Sep-26		6	Tishrei
21-Sep-26	Sabbath	7	Tishrei
22-Sep-26		8	Tishrei
23-Sep-26		9	Tishrei
24-Sep-26	Day of Atonement	10	Tishrei
25-Sep-26		11	Tishrei
26-Sep-26		12	Tishrei
27-Sep-26		13	Tishrei
28-Sep-26	Sabbath	14	Tishrei
29-Sep-26	1st Day of Feast of Booths	15	Tishrei
30-Sep-26	2nd Day of Feast of Booths	16	Tishrei
01-Oct-26	3rd Day of Feast of Booths	17	Tishrei
02-Oct-26	4th Day of Feast of Booths	18	Tishrei
03-Oct-26	5th Day of Feast of Booths	19	Tishrei
04-Oct-26	6th Day of Feast of Booths	20	Tishrei
05-Oct-26	7th Day of FOB/Sabbath	21	Tishrei
06-Oct-26	Eighth Day	22	Tishrei
07-Oct-26		23	Tishrei
08-Oct-26		24	Tishrei
09-Oct-26		25	Tishrei
10-Oct-26		26	Tishrei
11-Oct-26		27	Tishrei
12-Oct-26	Sabbath	28	Tishrei
13-Oct-26		29	Tishrei
14-Oct-26		30	Tishrei
15-Oct-26	New Moon Sabbath	1	Cheshvan
16-Oct-26		2	Cheshvan
17-Oct-26		3	Cheshvan
18-Oct-26		4	Cheshvan
19-Oct-26	Sabbath	5	Cheshvan

20-Oct-26		6	Cheshvan
21-Oct-26		7	Cheshvan
22-Oct-26		8	Cheshvan
23-Oct-26		9	Cheshvan
24-Oct-26		10	Cheshvan
25-Oct-26		11	Cheshvan
26-Oct-26	Sabbath	12	Cheshvan
27-Oct-26		13	Cheshvan
28-Oct-26		14	Cheshvan
29-Oct-26		15	Cheshvan
30-Oct-26		16	Cheshvan
31-Oct-26		17	Cheshvan
01-Nov-26		18	Cheshvan
02-Nov-26	Sabbath	19	Cheshvan
03-Nov-26		20	Cheshvan
04-Nov-26		21	Cheshvan
05-Nov-26		22	Cheshvan
06-Nov-26		23	Cheshvan
07-Nov-26		24	Cheshvan
08-Nov-26		25	Cheshvan
09-Nov-26	Sabbath	26	Cheshvan
10-Nov-26		27	Cheshvan
11-Nov-26		28	Cheshvan
12-Nov-26		29	Cheshvan
13-Nov-26		30	Cheshvan
14-Nov-26	New Moon Sabbath	1	Kislev
15-Nov-26		2	Kislev
16-Nov-26		3	Kislev
17-Nov-26	Sabbath	4	Kislev
18-Nov-26		5	Kislev
19-Nov-26		6	Kislev
20-Nov-26		7	Kislev

Date		Day #	Month
21-Nov-26		8	Kislev
22-Nov-26		9	Kislev
23-Nov-26		10	Kislev
24-Nov-26	Sabbath	11	Kislev
25-Nov-26		12	Kislev
26-Nov-26		13	Kislev
27-Nov-26		14	Kislev
28-Nov-26		15	Kislev
29-Nov-26		16	Kislev
30-Nov-26		17	Kislev
01-Dec-26	Sabbath	18	Kislev
02-Dec-26		19	Kislev
03-Dec-26		20	Kislev
04-Dec-26		21	Kislev
05-Dec-26		22	Kislev
06-Dec-26		23	Kislev
07-Dec-26		24	Kislev
08-Dec-26	Sabbath + Hannukah	25	Kislev
09-Dec-26		26	Kislev
10-Dec-26		27	Kislev
11-Dec-26		28	Kislev
12-Dec-26		29	Kislev
13-Dec-26	New Moon Sabbath	1	Tevet
14-Dec-26		2	Tevet
15-Dec-26	Sabbath	3	Tevet
16-Dec-26		4	Tevet
17-Dec-26		5	Tevet
18-Dec-26		6	Tevet
19-Dec-26		7	Tevet
20-Dec-26		8	Tevet
21-Dec-26		9	Tevet
22-Dec-26	Sabbath	10	Tevet

23-Dec-26			11	Tevet
24-Dec-26			12	Tevet
25-Dec-26			13	Tevet
26-Dec-26			14	Tevet
27-Dec-26			15	Tevet
28-Dec-26			16	Tevet
29-Dec-26		Sabbath	17	Tevet
30-Dec-26			18	Tevet
31-Dec-26			19	Tevet
01-Jan-27			20	Tevet
02-Jan-27			21	Tevet
03-Jan-27			22	Tevet
04-Jan-27			23	Tevet
05-Jan-27		Sabbath	24	Tevet
06-Jan-27			25	Tevet
07-Jan-27			26	Tevet
08-Jan-27			27	Tevet
09-Jan-27			28	Tevet
10-Jan-27			29	Tevet
11-Jan-27			30	Tevet
12-Jan-27		New Moon Sabbath	1	Shevat
13-Jan-27			2	Shevat
14-Jan-27			3	Shevat
15-Jan-27			4	Shevat
16-Jan-27			5	Shevat
17-Jan-27			6	Shevat
18-Jan-27			7	Shevat
19-Jan-27		Sabbath	8	Shevat
20-Jan-27			9	Shevat
21-Jan-27			10	Shevat
22-Jan-27			11	Shevat
23-Jan-27			12	Shevat

Date	Event	Day	Month
24-Jan-27		13	Shevat
25-Jan-27		14	Shevat
26-Jan-27	Sabbath	15	Shevat
27-Jan-27		16	Shevat
28-Jan-27		17	Shevat
29-Jan-27		18	Shevat
30-Jan-27		19	Shevat
31-Jan-27		20	Shevat
01-Feb-27		21	Shevat
02-Feb-27	Sabbath	22	Shevat
03-Feb-27		23	Shevat
04-Feb-27		24	Shevat
05-Feb-27		25	Shevat
06-Feb-27		26	Shevat
07-Feb-27		27	Shevat
08-Feb-27		28	Shevat
09-Feb-27	Sabbath	29	Shevat
10-Feb-27		30	Shevat
11-Feb-27	New Moon Sabbath	1	Adar
12-Feb-27		2	Adar
13-Feb-27		3	Adar
14-Feb-27		4	Adar
15-Feb-27		5	Adar
16-Feb-27	Sabbath	6	Adar
17-Feb-27		7	Adar
18-Feb-27		8	Adar
19-Feb-27		9	Adar
20-Feb-27		10	Adar
21-Feb-27		11	Adar
22-Feb-27		12	Adar
23-Feb-27	Sabbath	13	Adar
24-Feb-27	Purim	14	Adar

Date			Day	Month
25-Feb-27			15	Adar
26-Feb-27			16	Adar
27-Feb-27			17	Adar
28-Feb-27			18	Adar
01-Mar-27			19	Adar
02-Mar-27		Sabbath	20	Adar
03-Mar-27			21	Adar
04-Mar-27			22	Adar
05-Mar-27			23	Adar
06-Mar-27			24	Adar
07-Mar-27			25	Adar
08-Mar-27			26	Adar
09-Mar-27		Sabbath	27	Adar
10-Mar-27			28	Adar
11-Mar-27			29	Adar
12-Mar-27			30	Adar
13-Mar-27		New Moon Sabbath	1	Adar II
14-Mar-27			2	Adar II
15-Mar-27			3	Adar II
16-Mar-27		Sabbath	4	Adar II
17-Mar-27			5	Adar II
18-Mar-27			6	Adar II
19-Mar-27			7	Adar II
20-Mar-27			8	Adar II
21-Mar-27			9	Adar II
22-Mar-27			10	Adar II
23-Mar-27		Sabbath	11	Adar II
24-Mar-27			12	Adar II
25-Mar-27			13	Adar II
26-Mar-27			14	Adar II
27-Mar-27			15	Adar II
28-Mar-27			16	Adar II

29-Mar-27			17	Adar II
30-Mar-27		Sabbath	18	Adar II
31-Mar-27			19	Adar II
01-Apr-27			20	Adar II
02-Apr-27			21	Adar II
03-Apr-27			22	Adar II
04-Apr-27			23	Adar II
05-Apr-27			24	Adar II
06-Apr-27		Sabbath	25	Adar II
07-Apr-27			26	Adar II
08-Apr-27			27	Adar II
09-Apr-27			28	Adar II
10-Apr-27			29	Adar II
11-Apr-27		New Year New Month Reset Sabbath	1	Nisan
12-Apr-27			2	Nisan
13-Apr-27			3	Nisan
14-Apr-27			4	Nisan
15-Apr-27			5	Nisan
16-Apr-27			6	Nisan
17-Apr-27			7	Nisan
18-Apr-27		Sabbath	8	Nisan
19-Apr-27			9	Nisan
20-Apr-27			10	Nisan
21-Apr-27			11	Nisan
22-Apr-27			12	Nisan
23-Apr-27			13	Nisan
24-Apr-27		Passover	14	Nisan
25-Apr-27		1st Day of Unleavened Bread	15	Nisan
26-Apr-27		Day of First Fruits	16	Nisan
27-Apr-27		3rd Day of Unleavened Bread	17	Nisan
28-Apr-27		4th Day of Unleavened Bread	18	Nisan
29-Apr-27		5th Day of Unleavened Bread	19	Nisan

Date				
30-Apr-27		6th Day of Unleavened Bread	20	Nisan
01-May-27		7th Day of Unleavened Bread	21	Nisan
02-May-27	1	Sabbath	22	Nisan
03-May-27			23	Nisan
04-May-27			24	Nisan
05-May-27			25	Nisan
06-May-27			26	Nisan
07-May-27			27	Nisan
08-May-27			28	Nisan
09-May-27	2	Sabbath	29	Nisan
10-May-27		New Month Sabbath	1	Iyar
11-May-27			2	Iyar
12-May-27			3	Iyar
13-May-27			4	Iyar
14-May-27			5	Iyar
15-May-27			6	Iyar
16-May-27	3	Sabbath	7	Iyar
17-May-27			8	Iyar
18-May-27			9	Iyar
19-May-27			10	Iyar
20-May-27			11	Iyar
21-May-27			12	Iyar
22-May-27			13	Iyar
23-May-27	4	Sabbath	14	Iyar
24-May-27			15	Iyar
25-May-27			16	Iyar
26-May-27			17	Iyar
27-May-27			18	Iyar
28-May-27			19	Iyar
29-May-27			20	Iyar
30-May-27	5	Sabbath	21	Iyar
31-May-27			22	Iyar

Date			Day	Month
01-Jun-27			23	Iyar
02-Jun-27			24	Iyar
03-Jun-27			25	Iyar
04-Jun-27			26	Iyar
05-Jun-27			27	Iyar
06-Jun-27	6	Sabbath	28	Iyar
07-Jun-27			29	Iyar
08-Jun-27			30	Iyar
09-Jun-27		New Month Sabbath	1	Sivan
10-Jun-27			2	Sivan
11-Jun-27			3	Sivan
12-Jun-27			4	Sivan
13-Jun-27	7	Sabbath	5	Sivan
14-Jun-27	1		6	Sivan
15-Jun-27	2		7	Sivan
16-Jun-27	3		8	Sivan
17-Jun-27	4		9	Sivan
18-Jun-27	5		10	Sivan
19-Jun-27	6		11	Sivan
20-Jun-27	7	Sabbath	12	Sivan
21-Jun-27	8		13	Sivan
22-Jun-27	9		14	Sivan
23-Jun-27	10		15	Sivan
24-Jun-27	11		16	Sivan
25-Jun-27	12		17	Sivan
26-Jun-27	13		18	Sivan
27-Jun-27	14	Sabbath	19	Sivan
28-Jun-27	15		20	Sivan
29-Jun-27	16		21	Sivan
30-Jun-27	17		22	Sivan
01-Jul-27	18		23	Sivan
02-Jul-27	19		24	Sivan

03-Jul-27	20		25	Sivan
04-Jul-27	21	Sabbath	26	Sivan
05-Jul-27	22		27	Sivan
06-Jul-27	23		28	Sivan
07-Jul-27	24		29	Sivan
08-Jul-27	25	New Moon Sabbath	1	Rose
09-Jul-27	26		2	Rose
10-Jul-27	27		3	Rose
11-Jul-27	28	Sabbath	4	Rose
12-Jul-27	29		5	Rose
13-Jul-27	30		6	Rose
14-Jul-27	31		7	Rose
15-Jul-27	32		8	Rose
16-Jul-27	33		9	Rose
17-Jul-27	34		10	Rose
18-Jul-27	35	Sabbath	11	Rose
19-Jul-27	36		12	Rose
20-Jul-27	37		13	Rose
21-Jul-27	38		14	Rose
22-Jul-27	39		15	Rose
23-Jul-27	40		16	Rose
24-Jul-27	41		17	Rose
25-Jul-27	42	Sabbath	18	Rose
26-Jul-27	43		19	Rose
27-Jul-27	44		20	Rose
28-Jul-27	45		21	Rose
29-Jul-27	46		22	Rose
30-Jul-27	47		23	Rose
31-Jul-27	48		24	Rose
01-Aug-27	49	Sabbath	25	Rose
02-Aug-27	50		26	Rose
03-Aug-27		Feast of Weeks	27	Rose

YESHUATEKANI

04-Aug-27		28	Rose
05-Aug-27		29	Rose
06-Aug-27	New Moon Sabbath	1	Av
07-Aug-27		2	Av
08-Aug-27	Sabbath	3	Av
09-Aug-27		4	Av
10-Aug-27		5	Av
11-Aug-27		6	Av
12-Aug-27		7	Av
13-Aug-27		8	Av
14-Aug-27		9	Av
15-Aug-27	Sabbath	10	Av
16-Aug-27		11	Av
17-Aug-27		12	Av
18-Aug-27		13	Av
19-Aug-27		14	Av
20-Aug-27		15	Av
21-Aug-27		16	Av
22-Aug-27	Sabbath	17	Av
23-Aug-27		18	Av
24-Aug-27		19	Av
25-Aug-27		20	Av
26-Aug-27		21	Av
27-Aug-27		22	Av
28-Aug-27		23	Av
29-Aug-27	Sabbath	24	Av
30-Aug-27		25	Av
31-Aug-27		26	Av
01-Sep-27		27	Av
02-Sep-27		28	Av
03-Sep-27		29	Av
04-Sep-27		30	Av

05-Sep-27	New Moon Sabbath	1	Elul
06-Sep-27		2	Elul
07-Sep-27		3	Elul
08-Sep-27		4	Elul
09-Sep-27		5	Elul
10-Sep-27		6	Elul
11-Sep-27		7	Elul
12-Sep-27	Sabbath	8	Elul
13-Sep-27		9	Elul
14-Sep-27		10	Elul
15-Sep-27		11	Elul
16-Sep-27		12	Elul
17-Sep-27		13	Elul
18-Sep-27		14	Elul
19-Sep-27	Sabbath	15	Elul
20-Sep-27		16	Elul
21-Sep-27		17	Elul
22-Sep-27		18	Elul
23-Sep-27		19	Elul
24-Sep-27		20	Elul
25-Sep-27		21	Elul
26-Sep-27	Sabbath	22	Elul
27-Sep-27		23	Elul
28-Sep-27		24	Elul
29-Sep-27		25	Elul
30-Sep-27		26	Elul
01-Oct-27		27	Elul
02-Oct-27		28	Elul
03-Oct-27	Sabbath	29	Elul
04-Oct-27	The Day of Trumpets	1	Tishrei
05-Oct-27		2	Tishrei
06-Oct-27		3	Tishrei

07-Oct-27		4	Tishrei
08-Oct-27		5	Tishrei
09-Oct-27		6	Tishrei
10-Oct-27	Sabbath	7	Tishrei
11-Oct-27		8	Tishrei
12-Oct-27		9	Tishrei
13-Oct-27	Day of Atonement	10	Tishrei
14-Oct-27		11	Tishrei
15-Oct-27		12	Tishrei
16-Oct-27		13	Tishrei
17-Oct-27	Sabbath	14	Tishrei
18-Oct-27	1st Day of Feast of Booths	15	Tishrei
19-Oct-27	2nd Day of Feast of Booths	16	Tishrei
20-Oct-27	3rd Day of Feast of Booths	17	Tishrei
21-Oct-27	4th Day of Feast of Booths	18	Tishrei
22-Oct-27	5th Day of Feast of Booths	19	Tishrei
23-Oct-27	6th Day of Feast of Booths	20	Tishrei
24-Oct-27	7th Day of FOB/Sabbath	21	Tishrei
25-Oct-27	Eighth Day	22	Tishrei
26-Oct-27		23	Tishrei
27-Oct-27		24	Tishrei
28-Oct-27		25	Tishrei
29-Oct-27		26	Tishrei
30-Oct-27		27	Tishrei
31-Oct-27	Sabbath	28	Tishrei
01-Nov-27		29	Tishrei
02-Nov-27		30	Tishrei
03-Nov-27	New Moon Sabbath	1	Cheshvan
04-Nov-27		2	Cheshvan
05-Nov-27		3	Cheshvan
06-Nov-27		4	Cheshvan
07-Nov-27	Sabbath	5	Cheshvan

08-Nov-27			6	Cheshvan
09-Nov-27			7	Cheshvan
10-Nov-27			8	Cheshvan
11-Nov-27			9	Cheshvan
12-Nov-27			10	Cheshvan
13-Nov-27			11	Cheshvan
14-Nov-27		Sabbath	12	Cheshvan
15-Nov-27			13	Cheshvan
16-Nov-27			14	Cheshvan
17-Nov-27			15	Cheshvan
18-Nov-27			16	Cheshvan
19-Nov-27			17	Cheshvan
20-Nov-27			18	Cheshvan
21-Nov-27		Sabbath	19	Cheshvan
22-Nov-27			20	Cheshvan
23-Nov-27			21	Cheshvan
24-Nov-27			22	Cheshvan
25-Nov-27			23	Cheshvan
26-Nov-27			24	Cheshvan
27-Nov-27			25	Cheshvan
28-Nov-27		Sabbath	26	Cheshvan
29-Nov-27			27	Cheshvan
30-Nov-27			28	Cheshvan
01-Dec-27			29	Cheshvan
02-Dec-27		New Moon Sabbath	1	Kislev
03-Dec-27			2	Kislev
04-Dec-27			3	Kislev
05-Dec-27		Sabbath	4	Kislev
06-Dec-27			5	Kislev
07-Dec-27			6	Kislev
08-Dec-27			7	Kislev
09-Dec-27			8	Kislev

10-Dec-27		9	Kislev
11-Dec-27		10	Kislev
12-Dec-27	Sabbath	11	Kislev
13-Dec-27		12	Kislev
14-Dec-27		13	Kislev
15-Dec-27		14	Kislev
16-Dec-27		15	Kislev
17-Dec-27		16	Kislev
18-Dec-27		17	Kislev
19-Dec-27	Sabbath	18	Kislev
20-Dec-27		19	Kislev
21-Dec-27		20	Kislev
22-Dec-27		21	Kislev
23-Dec-27		22	Kislev
24-Dec-27		23	Kislev
25-Dec-27		24	Kislev
26-Dec-27	Sabbath + Hannukah	25	Kislev
27-Dec-27		26	Kislev
28-Dec-27		27	Kislev
29-Dec-27		28	Kislev
30-Dec-27		29	Kislev
31-Dec-27		30	Kislev
01-Jan-28	New Moon Sabbath	1	Tevet
02-Jan-28	Sabbath	2	Tevet
03-Jan-28		3	Tevet
04-Jan-28		4	Tevet
05-Jan-28		5	Tevet
06-Jan-28		6	Tevet
07-Jan-28		7	Tevet
08-Jan-28		8	Tevet
09-Jan-28	Sabbath	9	Tevet
10-Jan-28		10	Tevet

11-Jan-28			11	Tevet
12-Jan-28			12	Tevet
13-Jan-28			13	Tevet
14-Jan-28			14	Tevet
15-Jan-28			15	Tevet
16-Jan-28		Sabbath	16	Tevet
17-Jan-28			17	Tevet
18-Jan-28			18	Tevet
19-Jan-28			19	Tevet
20-Jan-28			20	Tevet
21-Jan-28			21	Tevet
22-Jan-28			22	Tevet
23-Jan-28		Sabbath	23	Tevet
24-Jan-28			24	Tevet
25-Jan-28			25	Tevet
26-Jan-28			26	Tevet
27-Jan-28			27	Tevet
28-Jan-28			28	Tevet
29-Jan-28			29	Tevet
30-Jan-28		Sabbath	30	Tevet
31-Jan-28		New Moon Sabbath	1	Shevat
01-Feb-28			2	Shevat
02-Feb-28			3	Shevat
03-Feb-28			4	Shevat
04-Feb-28			5	Shevat
05-Feb-28			6	Shevat
06-Feb-28		Sabbath	7	Shevat
07-Feb-28			8	Shevat
08-Feb-28			9	Shevat
09-Feb-28			10	Shevat
10-Feb-28			11	Shevat
11-Feb-28			12	Shevat

Date		Event	Day	Month
12-Feb-28			13	Shevat
13-Feb-28		Sabbath	14	Shevat
14-Feb-28			15	Shevat
15-Feb-28			16	Shevat
16-Feb-28			17	Shevat
17-Feb-28			18	Shevat
18-Feb-28			19	Shevat
19-Feb-28			20	Shevat
20-Feb-28		Sabbath	21	Shevat
21-Feb-28			22	Shevat
22-Feb-28			23	Shevat
23-Feb-28			24	Shevat
24-Feb-28			25	Shevat
25-Feb-28			26	Shevat
26-Feb-28			27	Shevat
27-Feb-28		Sabbath	28	Shevat
28-Feb-28			29	Shevat
29-Feb-28			30	Shevat
01-Mar-28		New Moon Sabbath	1	Adar
02-Mar-28			2	Adar
03-Mar-28			3	Adar
04-Mar-28			4	Adar
05-Mar-28		Sabbath	5	Adar
06-Mar-28			6	Adar
07-Mar-28			7	Adar
08-Mar-28			8	Adar
09-Mar-28			9	Adar
10-Mar-28			10	Adar
11-Mar-28			11	Adar
12-Mar-28		Sabbath	12	Adar
13-Mar-28			13	Adar
14-Mar-28		Purim	14	Adar

15-Mar-28		15	Adar
16-Mar-28		16	Adar
17-Mar-28		17	Adar
18-Mar-28		18	Adar
19-Mar-28	Sabbath	19	Adar
20-Mar-28		20	Adar
21-Mar-28		21	Adar
22-Mar-28		22	Adar
23-Mar-28		23	Adar
24-Mar-28		24	Adar
25-Mar-28		25	Adar
26-Mar-28	Sabbath	26	Adar
27-Mar-28		27	Adar
28-Mar-28		28	Adar
29-Mar-28		29	Adar
30-Mar-28	New Year New Month Reset Sabbath	1	Nisan
31-Mar-28		2	Nisan
01-Apr-28		3	Nisan
02-Apr-28		4	Nisan
03-Apr-28		5	Nisan
04-Apr-28		6	Nisan
05-Apr-28		7	Nisan
06-Apr-28	Sabbath	8	Nisan
07-Apr-28		9	Nisan
08-Apr-28		10	Nisan
09-Apr-28		11	Nisan
10-Apr-28		12	Nisan
11-Apr-28		13	Nisan
12-Apr-28	Passover	14	Nisan
13-Apr-28	1st Day of Unleavened Bread	15	Nisan
14-Apr-28	Day of First Fruits	16	Nisan
15-Apr-28	3rd Day of Unleavened Bread	17	Nisan

16-Apr-28		4th Day of Unleavened Bread	18	Nisan
17-Apr-28		5th Day of Unleavened Bread	19	Nisan
18-Apr-28		6th Day of Unleavened Bread	20	Nisan
19-Apr-28		7th Day of Unleavened Bread	21	Nisan
20-Apr-28	1	Sabbath	22	Nisan
21-Apr-28			23	Nisan
22-Apr-28			24	Nisan
23-Apr-28			25	Nisan
24-Apr-28			26	Nisan
25-Apr-28			27	Nisan
26-Apr-28			28	Nisan
27-Apr-28	2	Sabbath	29	Nisan
28-Apr-28			30	Nisan
29-Apr-28		New Moon Sabbath	1	Iyar
30-Apr-28			2	Iyar
01-May-28			3	Iyar
02-May-28			4	Iyar
03-May-28			5	Iyar
04-May-28	3	Sabbath	6	Iyar
05-May-28			7	Iyar
06-May-28			8	Iyar
07-May-28			9	Iyar
08-May-28			10	Iyar
09-May-28			11	Iyar
10-May-28			12	Iyar
11-May-28	4	Sabbath	13	Iyar
12-May-28			14	Iyar
13-May-28			15	Iyar
14-May-28			16	Iyar
15-May-28		**End of Time-Messiah Has Returned**	17	Iyar
16-May-28			18	Iyar

www.ingramcontent.com/pod-product-compliance
Lightning Source LLC
LaVergne TN
LVHW091535070526
838199LV00001B/71